"Navigating romantic relationships can be [...] when past traumas—big or small—affect [...] this guidebook, Melissa Fulgieri emphasizes the significance of recognizing these influences to foster healthier and more fulfilling relationships."

—**Rahim Rahemtulla, MD**, child, adolescent, and adult
psychiatrist in private practice in New York

"There is no checklist for healing trauma, Melissa Fulgieri reminds us, but there is now this wonderfully helpful book. Outlining the impact of relational trauma and guiding the reader toward healing, Fulgieri weaves together key elements of theory and self-guided practice in a gradual and demystified manner. We rarely know what harm we prevent by healing, she notes, but we can imagine. This book will help readers do their part."

—**Jackson Taylor, PhD**, clinical assistant professor
in the department of psychiatry at NYU Grossman
School of Medicine

"Melissa Fulgieri writes with the relatable tone of a human who has explored her own internal world, and an expert therapist who helps us explore ours. She makes the research on how child trauma impacts adult relationships accessible and relatable. Fulgieri offers embodied practices for addressing trauma triggers, while also driving home a key point: healing is not about perfection, but rather about reengaging with practices that bring you back to yourself, so that you can bring that full self to your relationships."

—**Lia Avellino, LCSW**, relational psychotherapist,
founder of Spoke Circles, and director of Head & Heart
at THE WELL

"Melissa Fulgieri masterfully combines cutting-edge research and actionable strategies to help readers rebuild trust and intimacy. A must-read for anyone committed to personal and relational growth."

—**Laura Caruso, LMHC,** NYC-based therapist and relationship expert, and host of the *Safe Space with Laura Caruso* podcast on Spotify

"Melissa Fulgieri's *Healing Relational Trauma* is a practical guide to understanding the effects of childhood wounds on current relationships. With insights and actionable tools, this book empowers readers to recognize their triggers and build self-awareness to foster deeper, healthier connections. It is a must-read for anyone ready to cultivate meaningful, authentic relationships and embrace healing—starting with themselves."

—**Francesca Reicherter**, founder of Inspiring My Generation Corporation; host of the *Normalize The Conversation* podcast; and author of six workbooks, including *You Are Not Alone*

Healing Relational Trauma

MOVE BEYOND PAINFUL CHILDHOOD EXPERIENCES
TO DEEPEN SELF-UNDERSTANDING AND
BUILD AUTHENTIC RELATIONSHIPS

MELISSA FULGIERI, LCSW

New Harbinger Publications, Inc.

Publisher's Note

This publication is designed to provide accurate and authoritative information in regard to the subject matter covered. It is sold with the understanding that the publisher is not engaged in rendering psychological, financial, legal, or other professional services. If expert assistance or counseling is needed, the services of a competent professional should be sought.

The examples outlined in this book are both imaginary and composite stories of clients' and other people's experiences. To maintain privacy and confidentiality, the names are made up and all identifying characteristics have been excluded or replaced.

NEW HARBINGER PUBLICATIONS is a registered trademark of New Harbinger Publications, Inc.

New Harbinger Publications is an employee-owned company.

Cover design by Amy Shoup

Acquired by Wendy Millstine and Jennye Garibaldi

Edited by Karen Schader

Library of Congress Cataloging-in-Publication Data on file

Printed in the United States of America

27   26   25

10   9   8   7   6   5   4   3   2   1   First Printing

To my sister, Allie, for being there the whole time as the other half who keeps our whole story.

To my niece, Lucy, whom we will create something new for.

Contents

Introduction

You may have picked up this book because you're worried that you simply aren't good at romantic relationships. Perhaps you feel something in your relationship is amiss or, as you navigate the dating world, you can't seem to get what you want or need from another. You might look back on your childhood fondly or think, *Sure, it wasn't perfect, but it wasn't terrible.* Maybe you vaguely remember some painful childhood experiences or maybe you remember very little about your childhood. You might be coming to this book with a combination of all these thoughts and feelings. Whatever the reason you are showing up to this book, there is likely far more to your backstory that is causing you to feel dissatisfied when it comes to romance. It is very possible you are moving through the world with invisible wounds from your upbringing that impact your current romantic relationships. Even if you walked away from childhood with no visible scars, there may have been small ways you were unable to get your emotional needs met as a kid. These wounds we carry and bring into our romantic relationships are called childhood relational trauma.

The word "trauma" may cause you to immediately bristle, thinking, *Trauma? Nope, not me. I had a roof over my head, good food to eat. I got presents during the holidays and for my birthday. My parents were there. Was it perfect? No. But it wasn't trauma with a capital T!*

Or maybe you're thinking, *Okay, yeah, I had one traumatic experience fifteen years ago. I put it past me, I'm over it. Why bring it up?*

Maybe you're thinking the exact opposite: *How am I ever going to move forward from what happened to me? Will I always feel this broken?*

For the purposes of this book, it doesn't matter how you classify your difficult childhood experiences. As humans, we like to categorize things to better understand ourselves and our world. However, when it comes to healing from trauma, it is not always helpful for us to do the scientific work of assigning a value to our experiences. Instead, I invite you to consider that any difficult, short, or prolonged relational experience you had during your formative years had an impact on the adult you became and the relationships you seek. Simply put, we all learn how to love by how we were loved, for better or worse.

Is This Book for You?

At this point, you may be wondering if you fall into the category of folks I am speaking directly to. That's a good question! Categorizing our past is extremely difficult, especially because our perception can be faulty.

If you're wondering whether this book is for you, I want to start by making clear that most of the time to be raised by humans is to experience some form of trauma. Author Mitch Albom (2003) writes: "All parents damage their children. It cannot be helped. Youth, like pristine glass, absorbs the prints of its handlers. Some parents smudge, others crack, a few shatter childhoods completely into jagged little pieces beyond repair." The Center for Addiction and Mental Health (n.d.) defines trauma as the lasting emotional response that often results from a distressing event. Who among us hasn't experienced something distressing in childhood and adolescence from a parent, teacher, relative, community member, or friend?

In the trauma world, we frame trauma as big "T" or little "t." Big "T" childhood relational trauma includes acute psychological trauma, like the death of a caregiver, and chronic relational trauma, like repeated abuse. Little "t" childhood relational trauma refers to events that don't include violence or abuse but do create significant distress. Both types of experiences can find welcoming support here.

Working with people over the course of a decade has made it abundantly clear to me that, if things weren't tough at home for you, they were tough at school, on the playground, at your neighbors' house, or your after-school program. Many of us, at one point during our upbringing, had one or more formative painful experiences interacting with important people, and we've carried these experiences with us into adulthood.

Although you may have experienced trauma in these other settings, this book is specifically about trauma you experienced from caregivers or parents. What makes childhood relational trauma pervasive and insidious are two things: our ability or inability to self-regulate when we go into survival mode following a traumatic experience and our environment's ability or inability to help and protect us from what we experienced.

Consider that you may have experienced a traumatic event at school and the way your parents responded made it worse. This counts as the type of trauma this book will focus on. In fact, trauma survivors often cite how their *environment* dealt with their trauma as the worst part of the trauma they experienced (Saxe, Ellis, and Brown 2015). For example, someone who experienced sexual abuse by their stepfather as a child may have been most negatively impacted by the fact that their mother didn't believe them when they disclosed the abuse.

Consider that the stories you remember about tough times growing up are the ones that have not only stayed with you in your memory but have also formed your identity and your choices. This book is less about erasing our painful past experiences but rather seeing them with new eyes, creating coping skills, and seeking out environments that support the healing of your wounds.

Why I Wrote This Book

Over my years as a therapist, I've worked with countless people whose lives have been affected by childhood relational trauma: families facing challenges like ineffective parenting, school truancy, addiction, and mental health issues; couples struggling with past trauma; and individuals striving to establish their identities and boundaries due to childhood trauma.

Realizing the prevalence of relational trauma impacting people's lives, I made it my mission to support those seeking healing, especially those without trauma diagnoses, by offering a trauma-informed approach. I want to help those seeking to heal their relational trauma understand that the way they were treated in childhood *does* matter, that those wounds *do* show up in adulthood, and it *doesn't* mean that they're broken or destined for unsatisfying relationships. Rather, they can harness the knowledge of their past to learn more about who they truly are as adults, in order to give and get what they need from themselves and their partners.

Our childhood relationships are our first foray into learning how to love and be loved. Because of the inevitable fallibility of being raised by imperfect people, many of us learned faulty ways of giving and receiving love. It is my sincere hope that this book will be a lighthouse for those of you who experienced difficult times being raised but weren't quite sure what to call it and so you also weren't quite sure what to do with it. This book will help you pinpoint the areas you need to heal that come from painful experiences within your childhood relationships, prioritizing both your pain *and* your healing. Just as I do with my clients in my private practice, I will help you build a strong self-knowledge that will guide you toward centering your authenticity, leaning into your vulnerability, identifying your triggers in the moment, and building the self-trust that will allow you to give yourself what you need so you can build and maintain the satisfying relationships you deserve.

What You'll Find Here

As we go, you will learn how to:

- take inventory of your emotions, thoughts, and behaviors that hinder your ability to give and receive the love you deserve in your relationship;

- overcome a tendency to invalidate your emotions by practicing self-compassion;

- build a mindful self-awareness practice to learn when you are invalidating your emotions and exhibiting other behaviors that lead to self-sabotaging true connection;

- soothe the fears that arise when you begin to unpack your past traumas;

- practice healing your wounded inner child that needs to be acknowledged and tended to;

- identify your triggers born from your deepest fears, wounds, and insecurities and understand how they surface in your current or past intimate relationships;

- use individual strategies to cope with and self-soothe those triggers;

- create an intentional network of support that is helpful and protective of your most vulnerable parts;

- practice relational skills so your partner(s) and loved ones can help you regulate, and learn how to do the same for them;

- determine if your needs are being met within your current relationship(s) and brainstorm ways to get more of those needs met.

At http://www.newharbinger.com/54384, you'll find a packet of tools and exercises for you to download. Some include space for your written responses; some have been included for your convenience in revisiting the content.

Your Healing Journey

Although therapy can be a life-changing tool, not all of us are privileged enough to have the resources that allow therapy to be readily accessible. You can use this book as a complement to your healing journey or on its own to gain a deeper understanding of yourself and your relationships. Either way, it will help you gain transformative knowledge about yourself—your wants and needs, your fears and insecurities, and how your past experiences impact your present thoughts, feelings, and behaviors—in order to give yourself more of what you need and help you get what you need from others.

I've learned from seeing clients over the course of a decade that there is no one-size-fits-all approach to healing trauma. This book offers integrative and eclectic strategies toward a path of relational healing. The skills draw from trauma-informed cognitive behavioral therapy, trauma system therapy, family systems theory, self-compassion and mindfulness-based practices, the Gottman method for couples therapy, and emotionally focused therapy for couples, among others. As I say to my clients, not all suggestions, tools, and strategies will work for you. You may even come up with your own strategies that work the best for you. Please remember to take what works and leave the rest.

Regardless of what ends up speaking to you, I see us as collaborating throughout this healing journey. I may be the expert in therapy, but you are the expert in your lived experience. My hope is that this book will empower you to better understand where your specific relational wounds are blocking you from making and sustaining the types of connections you desire and deserve. As we build this step-by-step process together, please remember that we all have our own unique strengths and resiliencies that we will call upon to tend to those wounds and fortify our relationship to ourselves and others. Don't believe me? Consider that it is your very strength, curiosity, and resiliency that led you to pick up this book in the first place.

CHAPTER 1

The Basics of Childhood Relational Trauma

In this book, I use "relational trauma" as an umbrella term that encompasses emotional abuse, physical abuse, sexual abuse, and emotional and/or physical neglect. The research suggests that many of us can connect our current relationship struggles to painful and difficult experiences in our upbringing (Levine and Heller 2010; Creasey 2002; DiLillo et al. 2009). The CDC found in 2018 that more than 60 percent of American adults experienced at least one adverse childhood experience (ACE), which includes all types of abuse, neglect, and other relational traumas that occur to people under the age of eighteen (Swedo 2023).

Examples of ACEs include exposure to physical, emotional, or sexual abuse or neglect; witnessing violence; serious mental illness; and substance misuse in the home. The more ACEs someone has had, the higher the risk for long-term negative effects on their learning, behavior, health, and mental health (Metzler 2017). Almost 25 percent of adults have experienced three or more ACEs, which is likely an underestimate due to underreporting. To determine your ACE score, head online to https://stopabusecampaign.org/take-your -ace-test.

Here's the kicker. When we don't process trauma, it stays in our body. In *The Body Keeps the Score*, psychiatrist and researcher Bessel van der Kolk (2014) points to how, even if the brain forgets what happened, the body remembers, and the consequences of that remembering are monumental. At least five of the ten leading causes of death are linked to having had a number of ACEs, shortening a person's life span by as much as nineteen years. ACEs can signal dangerous levels of stress, which derails brain development and increases risk for substance use, suicide, mental health conditions, heart disease, and dozens of other chronic illnesses (Merrick et al. 2019; Metzler 2017). Repeated exposure to stress in the absences of stable and nurturing relationships can lead to the body's activation of its stress response system. These changes to the brain can affect attention, impulsive behavior, decision making, learning, emotional regulation, and responses to stress in the future (Nelson et al. 2020). This research signaled something dire: if we do not take our healing into our own hands, it can have major consequences for our ability to live long and healthy lives filled with and bolstered by our enriching relationships. The good news is that suffering these prolonged consequences is preventable (Merrick et al. 2019).

During a phone call twenty-six years after Dr. Vincent Felitti (1998) created the ACEs study, I asked him what he believes most plagues our world as it relates to relational trauma. He answered immediately: *unintentional parenting*. Unintentional parenting means caregiving that doesn't take into account one's own worldview, cultural scripts, traumas, triggers, needs, and wants. When parents are unintentional, they project their feelings, needs, and desires onto their kids, which causes their kids to take on a parent's subjective experience and see that as their objective truth (Greene, Haisley, and Ford 2020). In turn, children grow into adults who take these subjective truths into their own relationships with others, which impacts how they interact with loved ones in adulthood.

The Messages of Relational Trauma

Here's an example of unintentional parenting impacting behavior as adults. Let's say that your mom grew up in poverty, and so she learned that she would need to finish every morsel of food on her plate because she never knew when her next meal would be. During your childhood, she instructs you to finish everything on your plate during mealtime, telling you that "there are little girls in the world less fortunate than you." Your mom is not conscious that the little girl she is talking about was her and that your childhood has far more resources than hers. As such, you grow into an adult who eats more than you need to feel full, because you learned that finishing everything on your plate marked the end of a meal.

What if your mom had healed from the trauma of an impoverished childhood that caused her scarcity mindset? She may have seen your childhood, with far more resources, as markedly different from hers, a childhood with scarce resources. Instead of unconsciously letting her parenting be guided by her past traumatic experiences, and acting from a place of fear and familiarity, she may have intentionally chosen a different way to parent.

While we wait for our society to implement widespread mindful parenting strategies, throughout the course of this book, we will learn and practice how to reparent yourself as an adult to get and give the love you need and deserve.

Without scars to point to, many who experience relational trauma have no idea that the many issues they experience as adults are attributable to their childhood. Unlike one major traumatic event like a car accident, relational trauma often happens over the course of time (Ferguson 2021). With any trauma, reminders of the past event trigger us in the present, as if the danger were happening again. When you have trauma resulting from a car accident, there are only so many reminders of the event—like the car you were driving, loud crashing noises, or the intersection where it happened.

With relational trauma, which is caused by the people in your life tasked with protecting you, traumatic reminders come from all kinds of sources—namely the relationships we have with ourselves and others (Herman 1992). In this way, the entire world becomes a dangerous place. The question becomes: how does one get a handle over the danger their body experiences when the world *itself* is triggering?

Many of us were not taught to understand our emotions as children, and, when we did show an emotion, we were told to stop feeling it. Instead of seeing our emotions, desires, and needs as normal, we learned to stifle them. Instead of seeing sadness, shame, or worry as part of the human experience, we learned to suppress those feelings or feel guilty or ashamed of feeling those ways. As we grew up, we took the invalidating messages we heard as children—"Don't cry or I'll give you something to cry about!" or "Stop being so shy and go give your uncle a kiss goodbye!"—and learned how to invalidate ourselves. These messages, now on repeat in our own minds, often prevent us from seeking help to better understand what happened to us and how it impacts us today.

Being traumatized is a normal response to an abnormal event. When something horrible occurs in your life, it is common to experience distress. Although we tend to pathologize people who are traumatized, the reality is, to be human is to experience trauma.

Trauma is subjective; that is, it is based on how someone experiences an event or series of events. The intensity and duration of someone's distress varies from person to person, trauma to trauma. An event becomes traumatic when it impacts our ability to cope and lead a fulfilling life. For instance, the same event, like a divorce, can impact two children differently. One child may experience the divorce as extremely traumatic and therefore more debilitating to their daily functioning, whereas the other child may experience it as less traumatic and therefore less debilitating (Rizvi and Najam 2014).

Many people believe they are broken or irrevocably damaged as a result of their past. If you've experienced trauma, please know that all hope is not lost. You can cultivate positive forces—for example, financial and community resources, social support, and healthy coping skills—that will support healing and minimize the effects of your trauma. Many therapists call these forces *protective factors*. However, *risk factors*, or the aspects of life that make healing more difficult, can both heighten trauma and make someone more susceptible to future traumatic events (Fereidooni, Daniels, and Lommen 2024). If you feel like you have few protective factors, don't despair! We will work on cultivating opportunities for protective factors and healing as well as identifying areas that you may not realize are strengths in the coming chapters. First, let's learn about childhood relational trauma and discover how it may be affecting your relationships as an adult.

Childhood relational trauma occurs following abuse, neglect, maltreatment, or abandonment from a caregiver to a child. The relational trauma may have contained attachment trauma, betrayal, or mistreatment from parents with personality disorders, such as narcissism (Tanasugarn 2022). Relational trauma is particularly damaging because the caregiver–child relationship sets the stage for children's future adult relationships as well as the characteristics and tendencies children adopt as they mature. Our first formative relationships have a major impact on our subsequent relationships, both the relationship that we build with ourselves and the ones we cultivate with others (Newport Academy 2017).

Common Causes of Childhood Relational Trauma

Growing up feeling consistently safe and cared for is crucial to developing a strong sense of self and cultivating supportive relationships.

This regular care helps us develop self-esteem and independence, along with other very important qualities, such as trust, effective communication, and emotional regulation, that help us transition into adolescence and adulthood. Childhood relational trauma occurs when we feel a lack of safety and/or love within our family of origin.

Relational trauma most often occurs over time instead of resulting from one big event, and it can be caused by one or multiple caregivers. Remember, you don't necessarily need to identify with having been abused by your parents to have childhood trauma that impacts you today. There is a high likelihood that your parents and caregivers weren't able to meet all of your needs (physical, emotional, psychological, spiritual, and creative, among others) all the time, which results in wounds that are still present today.

Prioritizing mental health only came into vogue nationally in the last few decades; previous generations were managing their own mental health alongside parenting today's adults. These days, while we know so much more about how parents' emotions and thoughts impact their behaviors, there is a very large group of folks who were parented by people who didn't have that knowledge. In fact, it is not so long ago that getting mental health support was seen as a weakness, barring many adults from getting the necessary support they required. An inability to obtain support may have resulted in many different types of relational trauma, including *abandonment, enmeshment*, and/or *abuse* within a close relationship.

Abandonment can take the form of physical or emotional neglect. Physical neglect is when a parent fails to provide for a child's basic needs, such as food, clothing, and shelter. Neglect may occur due to death, imprisonment, life-threatening or chronic illness, or divorce. Emotional neglect occurs when a caregiver regularly struggles to fulfill, disregards, or denies a child's need for acceptance, love, boundaries, and guidance. This can happen for a variety of reasons: caregivers may be overwhelmed with the needs of their other children, their partner, or their own aging parents; substance use, mental illness, trauma, or emotional immaturity may limit their ability to provide for a child's needs; or they may be preoccupied with outside stressors, including financial strain, work, or other activities and relationships.

Abandonment can occur in one experience, like a sudden death, or it can be an ongoing, chronic experience, such as a child often being left unsupervised or tasked with taking care of their younger siblings before they are developmentally ready to take on that responsibility.

Enmeshment is a lack of boundaries within the caregiver–child relationship. There are two types of enmeshment: a caregiver relying on a child to tend to their emotional needs, and a caregiver being overly involved in a child's life. Relying on a child to fulfill one's emotional needs creates problems because kids are naturally driven to satisfy their caregiver. This drive will often cause kids to meet their parents' needs at the expense of their own in order to receive love, praise, and acceptance. For example, you may have learned to act as your mom's best friend because you got praise when she confided in you, despite this role creating a wedge between you and your other family members.

A parent's overinvolvement during the transition to adolescence may cause teenagers to feel suffocated, disrupting their ability to form an independent, confident sense of self. This may look like a parent being overinvolved in a teenager's personal relationships, overinvolving their teen in their own emotional challenges, or being preoccupied with the safety and well-being of their teen to a detrimental level. It's important to note that each of the examples falling under enmeshment depends on a variety of factors, including a child's developmental level, cognitive level, and physical age. For instance, it's appropriate for a parent to help a child who is learning to use a toilet; however, a lack of bathroom boundaries with teenagers is not. That being said, broadly labeling parenting behaviors as wrong is unproductive as there are often a variety of factors to keep in mind, including lack of resources, mental health struggles, and discriminatory or oppressive systems.

Abuse may be emotional, physical, and/or sexual. Emotional abuse is a pattern of behavior that causes emotional distress, harms self-worth, and impacts emotional development. It can take many forms: rejection; constant criticism; threats; blaming the child for adult problems; dismissing the child's feelings; ridiculing, humiliating, or shaming them in public; calling them names; yelling or swearing at them; threatening to harm or abandon them; intimidating or intentionally scaring them to maintain power and control; gaslighting or manipulating them; ignoring or using silence to control their behavior; withholding love or support; or exposing them to domestic violence.

The definition of physical child abuse varies across state and country lines. Under the federal Child Abuse Prevention and Treatment Act (CAPTA), the US Department of Health and Human Services (Child Welfare Information Gateway 2022) defines child abuse and neglect as "any recent act or failure to act on the part of a parent or caregiver that results in death, serious physical or emotional harm, sexual abuse, or exploitation, or an act or failure to act that presents an imminent risk of serious harm."

Sexual abuse includes touching and non-touching abuse (http://www.preventchildabuse.org). CAPTA defines sexual abuse as "the employment, use, persuasion, inducement, enticement, or coercion of any child to engage in, or assist any other person to engage in, any sexually explicit conduct or simulation of such conduct for the purpose of producing a visual depiction of such conduct; or the rape, and in cases of caretaker or interfamilial relationships, statutory rape, molestation, prostitution, or other form of sexual exploitation of children, or incest with children." Non-touching abuse includes showing pornography to a child, trafficking a child, exposing a person's genitals to a child, encouraging a child to watch or hear sexual acts, and watching a child undress or use the bathroom.

Reading about the different types of abuse can be triggering, especially if certain behaviors resonate with your experience. Others may be thinking, *What kind of monsters do this to children?* Before we go completely villainizing parents and caregivers, it's important to note that it's common for parents and caregivers to be unaware of the harm they're causing, particularly with emotional abuse. Their behaviors may be unconscious and unintentional. In fact, trauma often occurs due to a parent's own childhood experiences, creating what is known as *generational trauma*, or trauma that repeats with each new generation (Greene et al. 2020; Felsen 2017). When a parent's trauma is left untreated, this type of distressing behavior often repeats with each new generation until a healthier way of parenting is learned and practiced.

Because relational trauma sometimes leaves no physical scars, many people are unaware that they were mistreated as children, and they grow into adults who have internalized their abuse as their fault, or "not that bad," or even "necessary." You may be replaying your own childhood memories to figure out where your experiences fall along the spectrum of trauma. Be gentle with yourself: it takes time to look at our past experiences with new eyes.

Clients have described this process as "coming out of a haze." Reviewing our past to center our truth is tough but necessary work. Until we take the brave step to label what has occurred as "traumatic," "dysfunctional," or even simply "unhelpful," patterns can repeat. It is helpful to remember that our caregivers may have been imperfect people with their own traumas and subsequent struggles that, without awareness and intentional effort, were passed on to us as children. This book does not require you to forget or forgive your caregivers for the harm they caused. It also doesn't require you to cut anyone out of your life, unless you feel that is necessary for your safety and well-being. All that is required is that you take the most important step toward your healing: acknowledging for yourself that harm occurred.

How Childhood Relational Trauma Impacts Our Adult Relationships

As we grow into adults and begin to seek love and connection in the form of intimate partnerships and other important relationships, we carry with us the wounds from our upbringing. The wounds we suffer from relational trauma and how they resurface in our current lives may not be easily recognizable. For example, let's say your grandfather, who raised you, would regularly call you lazy as you were growing up, beginning at age five into high school. Despite this treatment, you excelled in your classes and got into a prestigious university. As an adult looking back, you believe that you are over his name-calling, however you struggle to maintain a work–life balance and find difficulty putting boundaries in place at your job due to feeling as though you're never productive or studious enough. Even though you get regular accolades from your boss, you can't shake the feeling that if you cut back on your hours, your boss would find out how lazy you truly are. This has resulted in your relationship suffering as your wife often says she never feels prioritized over your job.

These relational wounds can show up in a variety of sneaky and not easily apparent ways. They may include a distorted sense of self, low self-esteem, overwhelming need for external validation, self-sabotaging behaviors, difficulty identifying emotions and needs, difficulty setting boundaries, social anxiety, withdrawn or avoidant behavior, difficulty regulating emotions, extreme neediness in relationships, manipulative behaviors, self-gaslighting, and difficulty ending unhealthy relationships (Bachert 2023; CPTSD Foundation n.d.; US Department of Veterans Affairs n.d.; Pharaon 2023; Bourbeau 2002).

If you struggle with these issues, it does not automatically mean that you experienced relational trauma as a child. And if you experienced relational trauma as a child, it does not automatically mean that you will struggle with any or all these things. Trauma is a deeply personal and subjective experience that impacts us all slightly differently. It's important to not make assumptions about ourselves and other people until we've done the deep work of self-reflection and making connections from our past to our present.

Without support and self-awareness, these wounds often cause conflict, miscommunication, strife, and dissatisfaction in our intimate adult relationships, especially when our wounds come into conflict with the wounds the other person in the relationship is carrying. A miscommunication may look like having an anger outburst when your partner says they think you're overreacting because it immediately and unconsciously takes you back to the many times your parents told you the same thing as you were growing up. You haven't made this connection yet—all your partner sees is you flying off the handle again, which reminds them of the violent outbursts their mother used to have, an experience that often led them to shut down and cower in fear. They have begun to do something similar in your relationship. Instead of shaming and blaming yourself or your partner, consider that you are both carrying wounds from the past that show up in the present in ways you have yet to understand. This is necessary work for both parties to do in order to heal.

When people fight in relationships, it's usually unclear what past pain got dredged up. This lack of awareness prohibits us from knowing how to make sure the same conflict doesn't repeat itself. Think about how many times you have gotten into the same fight with your partner or past partners. You each likely do a very similar dance each time, with little idea of how to break that frustrating pattern (Johnson 2004). Take the example you just read. Your partner says you're overreacting, you go from 0 to 60 and start yelling, and they shut down, afraid of your anger. This only causes you to get more angry and desperate to have your feelings acknowledged but it pushes them further away. This dance, currently happening on a weekly basis, ends with you both feeling hurt, disconnected, and dissatisfied. Without awareness of what occurred *within* each person, it is incredibly difficult to know how to get unstuck from the patterns that are triggering our childhood wounds. This lack of knowledge puts us at risk of repeating the same relational patterns from our childhood that created these wounds in the first place, thereby perpetuating a vicious cycle. In this book, you'll learn simple techniques for becoming more aware of your childhood wounds. These techniques will help you respond differently in your current relationships.

As you discover the role your childhood experiences play in your relationship issues, it's common to feel disbelief, cynicism, sadness, fear, anger, worry, frustration, confusion, or even numbness. Sometimes we perceive our childhood through rose-colored glasses. But the more you learn about trauma, the more you may begin to see how certain forms of caregiving were quite harmful to your sense of self.

On the other hand, it may feel affirming to learn that the very things you struggle with in your adult relationships did not arise out of thin air. Many of us tend to view our family life as "normal," until we learn that some behaviors and patterns were far more problematic and impactful than we originally thought. Remember: knowledge is power. Awareness of what happened to us is usually the first life-changing step toward healing.

If you're not aware of the wounds being triggered in your current relationship, it is incredibly difficult to know how to heal and get unstuck from unhealthy patterns. In certain cases, we seek out partners who aren't the best fit for us, but we still cannot seem to break the pattern of choosing the wrong people again and again. Or we ask our partners to fulfill needs that they simply are not able to because our request is coming from too deep a hole that was put there by our caregiver. At other times, we explode at our partner, get passive-aggressive, or completely shut down, feeling both justified and confused at why we behave like this. When we don't know what's coming up for us, we can experience so much stress and dissatisfaction in our relationships, without knowing a way to move forward productively. This book will help you gain the self-awareness required to enter into relationships from a grounded sense of self, armed with the knowledge of who you are and what you need.

Childhood Trauma vs. Adult Trauma

Now that we've connected childhood relationships to adult relationships, you may be wondering why we are talking only about how childhood trauma impacts our adult relationships and not delving into how adult traumatic experiences impact us. This is because trauma that happens in childhood has a totally different impact than trauma that occurs in adulthood. When a child experiences trauma, they can lock it away in their minds by *dissociating*, or creating parts of themselves where the trauma lives that they are not conscious of. When trauma happens to an adult, it is not as easily forgotten and therefore the memories cannot be locked away somewhere inaccessible. When we have traumatic experiences in childhood that we are no longer conscious of but that are still impacting our ability to move through the world in the ways we want to, work must be done to build awareness of how past experiences show up today and heal those parts of ourselves. When we don't build that awareness, we are destined to repeat these unhelpful patterns generation after generation.

Why Does Trauma Repeat?

Perhaps most frustratingly, the more trauma we've experienced, the more likely it is that we will experience trauma again. For example, survivors of childhood relational trauma have an increased risk of revictimization due to decreased self-worth, increased substance use, poor impulse control, and symptoms of depression (Culatta et al.

2020; Li, Zhao, and Yu 2019). I share this sobering reality not to depress you but to help you consider that the choices you've made in adulthood may have been predestined by the wounds you suffered in childhood.

It's one thing to not blame ourselves for what happened to us as children, but what about when we find ourselves in problematic situations and damaging romantic relationships as adults again and again? It is incredibly common for adults to blame themselves for their hardships, leading them to stay stuck under a blanket of shame. What they may not be considering is that their early experiences with trauma put them on a path to choose those situations again and again. In a study by psychologist David DiLillo and others (2009), trauma history was correlated with dysfunction and dissatisfaction in marital relationships due to lower levels of trust and poorer perceptions of relationship quality. In another study (Lahousen, Unterrainer, and Kapfhammer 2019), researchers found that insecure attachment resulted in more extreme perceptions of experiences including sensitivity to threats. This means that when a partner messes up, someone without trauma may see it as simply that: a mess up. If you have been traumatized and your partner messes up, you may more easily jump to "*See? This* is why I can't trust you! This is why I can't trust *anyone!*"

Repetition compulsions are when we unconsciously repeat trauma experiences we've had, only this time around, we are trying to do things differently by having an increased sense of control over the result. As psychoanalyst John Bowlby (1979a) put it, safety lies in familiarity. You may date conflict-avoidant partner after conflict-avoidant partner, not realizing that somewhere, deep down, you believe that if only you had tried a little harder in your last relationship, you could have gotten your past avoidant partner to open up more. You hope with this new partner, you will be successful. Or you date someone who cheats on you, and you are getting used to the feeling of being on edge, believing that this time around, you will be able to control the outcome by creating more rules and regulations around your new partner's comings and goings. You unconsciously think, *It will be different this time because I will do things differently!* In these cases, healing will come from knowing what we can and can't control in relationships. Ultimately, we can only control our *own* behaviors and perceptions in order to eventually lean in to have the vulnerable conversations about how we feel and what we need. This realization starts with considering that while these patterns may feel familiar, that doesn't mean they are enjoyable.

A Note on Healing and Control

One of the things I notice in the healing profession is that we often set our clients up to believe that they can control more than is actually possible. *Your boss is being mean to you? Think positive thoughts and you will get a promotion!*

Too often I find a lack of acknowledgement in the therapy space for the oppressive structures at play that no amount of positive thinking will shift. It's important to note that there are many hardships outside your control, one of which is how your parents treated you as a child. However, other risk factors that you cannot change, such as poverty, prejudice, and structural or relational racism, will absolutely make your trauma more insidious, debilitating, and pervasive. Research shows that Blacks; Hispanics; those with less than a high school education or with an annual income less than fifteen thousand dollars; people who are unemployed or unable to work; and those who identify as gay/lesbian or bisexual reported significantly higher exposure to adverse childhood experiences than comparison groups (Merrick et al. 2018).

As you go through this book, it is important to remember what you are and are not responsible for shifting. This book focuses on what you can control, alongside the understanding that depending on what privilege and power your identities hold or do not hold will impact your healing journey. I recommend reflecting on the protective forces in your life that helped outweigh your risk factors, building your resiliency. In this way, you can continually seek to rebalance the scales by building as many protective factors as possible in your life to offset the risk factors and marginalization that you are unable to change. These protective factors often fall under the areas of community, enjoyment, rest, and purpose.

The Pain of Not Being Seen

Many people struggle in their relationships but cannot point to a massive or chronic experience of childhood trauma that would be the smoking gun for all their relational problems as adults. Sometimes it's not so obvious why or how we walked away from our childhood with lasting wounds. However, the experience of not being understood, or even *seen* by your parents is deeply traumatic.

Remember that scene in *Titanic* when Rose is surrounded by people dining, dressed in exquisite clothes, regaled with all the food and riches one could ever want, and yet she couldn't be more unhappy? As people talk and laugh around her, no one seems to notice her profound loneliness or despair. Eventually she breaks away from the stifling environment, running toward the back of the boat intending to jump off, but before she does, she meets Jack, who, both effortlessly and for the first time, becomes the first person to ever truly *see* her.

This scene describes both how painful not being seen is as well as how incredible the opposite can feel. So many of us have experienced the deeply painful feeling of not being seen for who we truly are—whether that's by your father, who refused to respect that you chose a different career path than he did even though you love what you do; or your mother, who only wants to know when you're going to find a partner when you're desperate for her to ask you about your recent promotion at work; or your grandparents, who refuse to acknowledge that your partner is your romantic mate, not your friend, which they insist on calling them. The pain that comes from feeling unseen by those closest to us may be a universal experience, one that is not usually classified in psychological manuals as trauma.

Feeling unseen often occurs when our parents and caregivers have their own unprocessed trauma that impacts their parenting and are also experiencing generational and cultural divides. For example, your dad might not respect your career path just as *his* dad did not respect his career path. Instead of processing his grief and anger around that experience, he replicates the very same painful experience he endured as a young man. Sometimes we know what trauma our parents experienced; sometimes we can only sense that something is amiss but don't know what; and sometimes we are completely unaware. In the meantime, we are predisposed to gain our caregiver's approval, which requires us to create two separate realities: the reality where we align ourselves with our caregiver's expectations and a confusing private reality where, as John Bowlby (1979b) writes, "We know what we are not supposed to know and feel what we are not supposed to feel."

As children, we cannot see our parents as fully human creatures who are subjective and fallible. Our developmentally self-absorbed childlike minds see our parents' mistakes as our fault, especially if that's how it's described to us by our caregivers (Piaget 1962). In fact, divorce counselors often tell parents to emphasize that it isn't their kids' fault that they are separating because kids often default to this understanding simply because at young ages, *everything* is about you.

It is only when we begin to see our parents as fully human at various stages of their own healing that we can ultimately look on our childhood experiences with critical eyes. This added context allows us to change the stories we tell about ourselves. *It wasn't because I was too needy, it was because my mom was a single parent, overwhelmed and unsupported. It's not because I am too sensitive; in my parent's culture, showing emotion isn't accepted.* In this way, learning about the traumatic impacts of being chronically unseen can be a game changer, both in healing from our past and also choosing to surround ourselves with people who make us feel seen, heard, and understood.

Identifying Childhood Wounds

Now that we know how painful it is not to have our experiences in childhood validated, let's identify our childhood relational wounds specifically so we can become more aware of them, which is the first step toward beginning to heal from them. Remember, wounds don't always have to come from malicious places but they can result in experiencing childhood relational trauma nonetheless. In fact, these wounds can get created even when parents are doing their absolute best.

This list of common childhood wounds has been adapted from Vienna Pharaon's (2023) *Origins of You: How Breaking Family Patterns Can Liberate the Way We Live and Love* and Lisa Bourbeau's (2002) *Heal Your Wounds and Find Your True Self.* You may find that you identify with one or more of these wounds. You may also notice that many of these wounds overlap in their characteristics and subsequent adult struggles. Identifying wounds that resonate with you will shed light on what was particularly difficult about your childhood and how that difficulty may present itself now in adulthood.

Worthiness wounds form when you grow up with conditional love. You may have felt like you needed to be perfect or excel at school or a sport in order to be loved. Because your value was dependent on something external, as an adult, you may now feel like you need to play a certain role in your relationships in order to be worthy of love. You may be struggling with perfectionism, low self-esteem, or low self-worth.

Belonging wounds can surface growing up in a family with a strict belief system that you don't fit into, perhaps causing you to identify as the black sheep of the family. You may have either faked it to fit in or rebelled against the status quo, leading to isolation. As an adult, you continue to feel like you don't quite fit in or that there's something wrong with you. You may be struggling with low self-esteem, low self-worth, feelings of disconnection, and loneliness.

Prioritization wounds come from not being made to feel important growing up. Your parents may have been overworked, been caregivers for others, struggled with substance abuse, or had a chronic illness taking up their attention, leading to you not feeling important enough in adult relationships. As an adult, getting canceled on or ghosted leaves you very upset. You might even struggle to respect others' boundaries due to needing frequent reassurance that you matter.

Trust wounds form when there is an absence of honesty or transparency in your childhood, such as being lied to or restricted from gaining information that directly impacts your well-being. This may have been around holding a big secret like a parent's infidelity or debt, or dealing with frequent broken promises from parents. In adult relationships, you may be the one who constantly feels on guard, checking your partner's text messages or waiting for a crisis to occur. On the other hand, you may keep walls up and be hyperindependent so you're never let down by others.

Safety wounds are associated with explicit abuse and neglect. If there was an overall lack of care and concern for your well-being, you may have built walls of protection to guard against further harm. In adulthood, this may look like a difficulty being vulnerable, or avoiding conflict to keep the peace.

Abandonment wounds come from losing a parent to death, debilitating illness, divorce, or incarceration, among other reasons. As an adult, you may fear being alone or not included in activities. You may fear that your partner will leave you and find yourself clinging to them. This can also look like hyperdependence or hyperindependence, also known as not leaning on anyone so ultimate abandonment won't hurt as much.

Guilt wounds occur if you were often guilt-tripped as a child as a way to get you to behave or do what your caregivers wanted. As an adult, this can make you feel afraid of setting boundaries or asking others to meet your needs for fear of being a burden. You may struggle with self-sacrificing and being overly accommodating or avoiding conflict.

Injustice wounds can arise from many places—experiencing childhood poverty, having overly critical parents with unreasonably high expectations, or emotionally detached parents who required you to suppress your emotions, among others. As an adult, this wound can make you deeply sensitive to experiences of injustice or unfairness or cause you to have difficulty with authority and fear control.

Notice the feelings that arise within you as you read through these wounds. Pay special attention to when you feel a sensation in your body or think to yourself, *That sounds like me.* You have begun to identify the type of wounds you carry. You may find it helpful to take ten minutes or so to write in your journal about what wounds resonated with you and why.

Putting It All Together

You've already learned so much about childhood relational trauma and how that may be showing up in your adult life. We've reviewed the different types of childhood relational trauma as well as common causes. You've learned how childhood relational trauma impacts . people later on in life. You've learned about how childhood trauma impacts us differently than trauma we've experienced as adults.

You've gained knowledge around how trauma repeats in families, generation after generation, and how awareness is the first step to stopping that cycle from continuing.

You've started to do some reflecting on which childhood relational wounds resonate most with you. Next, we're going to dive into how our past, along with our childhood wounds, shapes our present by learning more about how trauma manifests in our bodies and minds.

CHAPTER 2

How Past Trauma Shapes Our Present

This chapter will dig into the ways our past wounds impact our present thoughts, feelings, and behavior. We'll look at the psychological theories, neuroscience, and relational frameworks that help to explain *why* we do things in relationships that make us feel bad, misunderstood, and dissatisfied.

Go into this chapter with an open and curious mind. Try not to see this information as a prescriptive formula or perfect causation for why you, your partner, or your past partners are the way they are. Take what resonates with you and leave the rest. Ultimately, with deeper understanding and awareness of ourselves, we can begin to take the first steps toward making different choices.

An Overview of Stress Responses

The stress we experience from trauma brings us to a state of alertness that is controlled by ancient systems of the brain and body known as survival circuits (Saxe, Ellis, and Brown 2015; Guy-Evans 2023). When we are in danger, we experience a threat → react to the stimuli that is related to our survival → put that threat in context → and then we do something about that threat. What we do totally depends on if we are able to properly contextualize where this threat is coming from (Saxe, Ellis, and Brown 2015; Cleveland Clinic 2024). We'll talk more about this, but first let's consider the options of what we do when danger is present.

You may have heard the term *fight or flight*, which refers to our body's stress response when we're faced with danger. When our body releases hormones that prompt us to make a snap decision, we have some options: stay and *fight* or run and flee, also known as *flight*. This stress response is your body's way of automatically responding to keep you alive and safe. There are two other stress response options that are not as widely known: *freeze* and *fawn*. These are all sympathetic nervous system responses that, from an evolutionary perspective, date back to when our ancestors frequently faced life-or-death situations (Guy-Evans 2023).

Whichever stress response your body chooses when you're in conflict (keeping in mind that it may choose different responses for different situations), the overall goal of our stress response is to escape danger to return us back to our previously calm and relaxed state (Saxe, Ellis, and Brown 2015). If you've ever behaved in a certain way that confused you following a stressor, consider your stress response. As you read about these different stress responses (Guy-Evans, 2023; Cleveland Clinic 2024), reflect on which ones resonate with you.

A *fight* response suggests that your body is urging you to fight the danger. If you have a *fight* response, when you perceive danger, signals get sent to your brain from your body that help you gear up to attack. Signs of a fight response include:

- tight jaw and grinding teeth;

- an urge to punch someone or something;

- a desire to stomp or kick;

- a feeling of intense rage;

- crying out of anger;

- attacking the source of danger.

A *flight* response means your body is guiding you to run away from the danger. Your body produces adrenaline, signaling to prepare to run from your danger. Signs of a flight response include:

- restless body;

- feeling fidgety or tense;

- constantly moving or overexercising;

- dilated or darting eyes;

- feeling of numbness in your arms and legs.

Freeze causes your body to stay still, shut down, and not make any sudden movements to evade the danger. If you have this response, you may feel stuck in place. Freeze occurs when your body does not think you have an option to flee the situation or fight the predator. Imagine seeing a bear and having nowhere to escape but not being able to go head-to-head with it. Chances are, your body will choose to stay frozen in place, waiting out the danger until the bear passes you by. Signs of a freeze response include:

- decreased heart rate;

- loud pounding heart;

- sense of dread;

- feeling stiff, heavy, cold, or numb.

The fourth stress response is *fawn*, which urges you to please the source of your danger to avoid harm. This response occurs when the body does not believe it has another option or when other responses have proved unsuccessful. Fawning often occurs within people who grew up in psychologically and physically abusive households, or took on cultural scripts that required them to be "good" instead of authentic. In these situations, being helpful to the caregiver by tending to their needs (and suppressing or deprioritizing one's own needs) becomes the only means of survival. Fawning can look like:

- being overly agreeable;

- going above and beyond to try to make someone else happy, even to your detriment;

- missing your internal cues that you are angry, depleted, or frustrated;

- being preoccupied with the opinion of others;

- struggling to maintain or put in place boundaries;

- being easily controlled or manipulated.

When we think about frightening or dangerous situations, we may only conjure up scenes of outwardly or obviously scary experiences, like the split second before we get punched by a schoolyard bully or the unsettled feeling we have walking home alone late at night. However, with relational trauma, fear or danger can also be triggered by someone invalidating your feelings, ignoring your needs, or putting unrealistic emotional burdens on you, or by watching two people argue.

Stress responses are automatic responses that occur in our body when we are in danger, regardless of whether we are aware of them. In fact, we are very rarely aware of what choice our body is making when we are experiencing a stress response. How many times have you been in a fight, yelled your head off, said things you didn't mean, and when you felt calmer, had little or no idea what you said or exactly what went down? Chances are your stress response was activated and you responded automatically with little input from the part of your brain known for making rational, fully thought-out decisions (Saxe, Ellis, and Brown 2015).

Trauma and the Stress Response

Childhood relational trauma can leave us feeling unsafe in our own bodies. The trauma becomes imprinted on our minds and bodies, fundamentally changing how we respond to the outside world. Instead of our being on high alert when we face a predator or life-threatening external force, the fear of danger begins to live *within* us. Our body gets used to being on high alert as we walk through the world, responding to our present-moment experiences with information from the past. For example, someone who grew up in a chaotic household where violence was the main form of communication might interpret a rude look from a stranger on the subway as *He wants to fight me*, and their stress response steps in to help them prepare to fight. On the other hand, someone who grew up in a non-violent household may see that same person on the subway and instead think, *I wonder what his problem is!* before they calmly continue about their day.

Trauma bars us from being able to properly contextualize a threat between past and present. Whether you have big "T" or little "t," trauma can impact how you respond to a stranger's rude look. In the first example, this person experienced chronic abuse and is subsequently dealing with traumatic stress. As we saw, they had little to no control over the threat and their response, like a switch that gets flipped from off to on. Their flipped switch brought them back to being in their childhood environment, where a threat meant they would need to prepare for a fight. If you have little "t," in which your distressing childhood relational experiences didn't result in a survival-in-the-moment reaction, the impacts will be more subtle and largely related to your sense of self and the world. For instance, you might see that rude look and think to yourself, *Gosh, why does everyone seem to have a problem with me all the time?* This tendency for self-blame comes from your formative experiences of your parents being overly critical of you when they struggled to regulate their emotions. Because of their difficulties with emotional reactivity, you grew up thinking that their overreactions to your chores not being done properly was because you were careless and uncaring, which they would often tell you at the height of their frustration.

Trauma changes how we think about what we see, and subsequently, how we respond. Dr. Bessel van der Kolk (2014) puts it best: "Our brain is a cultural organ. Experiences shape our brain." When we've experienced past trauma, we're not only responding to our experience in the present, but we're also using messages from the pain in our past to guide our way of being. Consider someone who grew up being told how "good" they were in comparison to their needier sibling, who had behavioral issues. They learned that being the "good" kid was the way to make their parents happy. The only problem is, like any other kid, they also had hard days. However, they suppressed their negative emotions during hard days, and developed a fawning response by pretending everything was fine all the time, taking great pride in being the "easy" one. They learned that their self-worth was tied to how "good" and "nice" they were. As an adult, being upset or mad at someone feels deeply uncomfortable, even shameful, so they have become well versed at hiding negative feelings, pretending to be totally fine even if they are upset, hurt, or disappointed. They use passive aggression to get their needs met, making pointed comments to communicate any negative emotions. This is just one example of the many different ways you might have learned to deal with stress to get what you needed in your childhood environments. None of us escapes this dynamic—we all have an evolutionary drive to do what we have to do to get safety and comfort from our loved ones.

How We Relate to Our Earliest Caregivers

Attachment refers to the psychological and emotional bond developed between a young child and their caregiver. The theory, first developed by John Bowlby (1979a) and expanded upon by psychologist Mary Ainsworth (1989), reasoned that the ways we seek closeness to our primary caregivers during stressful situations set the foundation for how we navigate subsequent intimate relationships. Just like our stress responses, attachment theory is also evolutionary. Bowlby believed that our desire for our caregiver's love and presence as infants is just as important for our survival as our desire for food.

The way we think about and behave or "attach" in relationships is called our *attachment style*. Once we know our attachment style, we can predict, with stunning accuracy, how we will behave in adult intimate relationships, based on how we were raised (Levine and Heller 2010; Lahousen, Unterrainer, and Kapfhammer 2019). As you read about these styles (adapted from Robinson, Segal, and Jaffee 2024), think about which type resonates the most with you and which types remind you of your current or past partners.

Secure attachment: If you were consistently able to rely on your parents to fulfill your basic needs, you likely developed a secure attachment style. Securely attached kids feel loved, safe, understood, and comforted by their caregivers. Regularly getting needs met by a caregiver creates a strong belief that relationships are a safe space where one can be their true self. In essence, securely attached kids grow up to believe, at their core, that they are worthy of love.

Generally speaking, adults who are securely attached in relationships are able to:

- regulate their emotions;

- easily trust others;

- use effective communication skills;

- seek out emotional support when needed;

- find comfort in spending time alone;

- self-reflect and take accountability during conflict.

Insecure attachment: On the other hand, if you experienced inconsistent or rejecting caregiving growing up, it is more likely that you developed any one of the three insecure attachment styles: *anxious, avoidant,* or *disorganized.* In these cases, you may have learned through your experience relating to your early caregivers that close relationships do not necessarily get your emotional and psychological needs met. There are a variety of causes for insecure attachment including:

- inexperienced parenting;

- caregiver mental health;

- caregiver addiction;

- traumatic experiences;

- inconsistency or separation from primary caregiver;

- frequent moves or placements.

An *anxious attachment style*, also known as anxious-ambivalent or anxious-preoccupied, is characterized by a persistent fear of rejection or abandonment, and an overdependence on partners for validation, reassurance, or emotional regulation. This style often develops from having an inconsistent caregiver who was not attuned to your needs as a child.

If this style resonates with you, your caregiver might have:

- vacillated between being overly attached to and detached from you;

- been easily overwhelmed;

- been attentive to your needs at times and rejecting of your needs at other times;

- made you responsible for holding and tending to their feelings, often at the expense of your own.

These are signs that you may have an anxious attachment style in relationships:

tendency to be clingy or overly needy;

high sensitivity to criticism;

consistent need for approval, validation, or reassurance;

difficulty spending time alone;

feeling unworthy of love and/or low self-esteem;

debilitating fear of rejection or abandonment.

An *avoidant attachment style*, also known as dismissive-avoidant, is marked by a failure or difficulty in building long-term relationships with others due to an inability to engage in physical or emotional intimacy. This style develops when one has emotionally distant, absent, or rigidly strict caregivers.

If this style resonates with you, your caregiver might have:

- been slow to respond to your needs;

- rejected your expression of needs or emotions;

- reprimanded you for depending on them;

- expected you to be independent or left you to fend for yourself.

These signs indicate that you may have an avoidant attachment style:

strong sense of independence;

persistent avoidance of intimacy;

discomfort with expressing feelings;

hard time trusting others;

preoccupation with not wanting to be trapped in relationships.

A *disorganized attachment style,* also known as fearful-avoidant, is characterized by intense fear leading to disorganized behavior (Main and Solomon 1990). This style most often develops when there is abuse or neglect present during childhood.

If this style resonates with you, your caregiver might have:

- had an extremely inconsistent or random parenting behaviors;

- been abusive or neglectful;

- been struggling with addiction or debilitating mental health concerns;

- fostered a sense of fear in your upbringing.

These signs indicate that you may have a disorganized attachment style:

finding relationships confusing or unsettling;

swinging between emotional extremes or contradictory behaviors;

difficulty trusting others;

signs of both avoidant and anxious attachment.

It is important to remember that while there are neglectful parents out there, many parents are busy providing financially or preoccupied with other parts of child-rearing, such as maintaining a clean household or ensuring a child's academic success. In fact, there are many reasons why even conscious and well-meaning parents might create insecurely attached children, including having a lack of financial and community resources.

There is a fair amount of overlap between these categories. If you are confused as to what style most closely resembles yours, don't worry! You're going to fill out an assessment to build self-awareness so you can further understand how you show up in relationships from an attachment perspective. Following the assessment, we'll do two exercises to support you in working *with* your attachment style.

Self-Awareness Attachment Quiz

Take this quiz (adapted from Levine and Heller 2010) to see what attachment style you have. The quiz is not a definitive tool, but it will be a first step toward building your self-awareness around how you attach to others. At http://www.newharbinger.com/54384, you'll find an exercise on self-acceptance to supplement this quiz.

True or False?

1. I find it difficult to get close to others.

2. Others want me to be more intimate than I am comfortable being.

3. I find it difficult to completely trust others.

4. Being independent is very important to me.

5. I have a hard time leaning into conflict with loved ones.

6. I struggle to vocalize my thoughts and feelings.

7. I have been called emotionally distant or unavailable.

8. I find it difficult to depend on others.

9. I worry about being abandoned by others.

10. When a loved one pulls away, I worry that it is because I have done something wrong.

11. I usually want more intimacy and closeness than others do.

12. I worry others will hurt me by ending our relationship.

13. I am very uncomfortable, or completely avoid, being alone.

14. I am sensitive to how others feel and act.

15. I struggle with people pleasing.

16. I have a need for frequent validation.

The more you answered "True" to statements 1–8, the more likely it is that you have an avoidant attachment style. The more you answered "True" to statements 9–16, the more likely it is that you have an anxious attachment style. The more you answered "True" across both sections, the more likely it is that you have a disorganized attachment style. The more "False" statements you have overall, the more likely it is that you have a secure attachment style.

How Attachment Surfaces In Romantic Relationships

Knowing your attachment style can be incredibly helpful in understanding how you behave in your romantic relationships (Simpson, Rholes, and Phillips 1996). Do you shut down during conflict with your partner, and, experiencing a strong urge to flee, pack an overnight bag? Or, when your partner leaves on a business trip, do you think through all the worst-case scenarios your mind can come up with: *Maybe they forgot about me! Maybe they'll meet someone they like better!* These relationship tendencies are likely related to your attachment style along with relational trauma.

When we begin to form intimate adult relationships, we unconsciously start to expect our romantic partners to act as our parents did, for better or worse. In preparation for our childhood patterns to repeat, we think and act in prescribed ways, called *internal working models* (Bowlby 1979a), often creating self-fulfilling prophecies.

Understanding Ourselves, Others, and the World

When children grow up feeling safe with a caregiver, they start to use them as a secure base to come back to as they begin to go out and explore the world. This relationship gives children confidence to take risks, experiment, make mistakes, and create a sense of self that is separate from their caregiver. The experience of exploring and returning is influenced by the caregiver's responses, which ultimately create patterns of attachment for the child (Bowlby 1979a). As this child grows up, these patterns then create internal working models that guide their feelings, thoughts, and expectations in later intimate relationships. These models dictate a person's self-worth and how they expect others will react to them. For example, if someone doesn't call after a first date, a securely attached person may be disappointed but may also consider that they simply weren't compatible and understand that mismatch of interest in dating is something that is likely to occur for all folks who date.

However, when we grow up with insecure attachment, the way we see the world, others, and ourselves mimics our learned avoidant, anxious, and disorganized patterns. These patterns become stable and self-fulling over time—they can predict how we'll interpret situations and what we'll do across a variety of scenarios (Levine and Heller 2010). An anxiously attached individual may respond to not getting a call after a first date by fearing that this rejection is a sign that they are unlovable and unworthy. Or an insecure person in a relationship might automatically assume that when their partner doesn't pick up their phone call, they must be mad at them. This assumption may harken back to when their mother used to give them the silent treatment for a transgression they didn't know they had committed. Consistently receiving the silent treatment as a kid created a working model in adulthood that says, "When people are unreachable, it's probably because they're mad at you."

Perhaps you grew up avoidantly attached, believing that your opinions and feelings didn't matter. In fact, you often heard your mother say, "Children should be seen and not heard." She seemed regularly aloof, was preoccupied with her own friendships, and rarely showed interest in your daily experiences—both positive and negative. (Sounds like a prioritization wound, right?) Now when your partner does something that upsets you, like forgetting to unload the dishwasher, you say nothing about it. Your internal working model is *My voice does not matter, my partner has no interest in how I feel*, so you automatically stay silent and suppress your feeling of frustration, distracting yourself with your favorite video game. When your partner continues to forget to unload the dishwasher, you see their behavior as further confirmation that you are right—what you need doesn't matter. The pattern repeats.

Here's another example. Let's say you had to tend to your stepfather's anxious behavior, often silencing your own needs from an early age in order to receive praise for helping your stepfather through his panic attacks. From these experiences, you learned that your self-worth was tied to helping people (a worthiness wound). As an adult, you find yourself getting involved with friends and partners who require you to be a caregiver to them. Even though this caregiving depletes you, it also makes you feel purposeful, enhancing your self-esteem. When your partner has an issue, you run to solve it for them, expecting them to want you to fix it for them.

EXERCISE: Self-Acceptance

Now that you have a better sense of your attachment style, visit http://www.newharbinger.com/54384 for an exercise to boost your self-acceptance. You'll be asked to write in detail about a time you got into a conflict with a current or past partner, including all the behaviors you can remember; to write down the feelings you had at each stage of this conflict; and to end by writing some words of acknowledgment, encouragement, and validation for how you felt during that conflict.

Remember to *validate how you felt, not what you did*. All feelings are valid; however, behaviors can range from helpful to unhelpful. When we say things to ourselves like *I just need to chill. I should just get over it*, we are actively making the situation worse because we are denying our emotional experience. The best way to tend to our emotional experience and actually move through it is to acknowledge that it exists with some self-acceptance.

Interaction Between Attachment Styles

Up until now, we've discussed attachment styles from only one side. But things can get complicated when two people are in a relationship, as they each have their own ways of being that come from their unique upbringings, including their attachment styles.

Remember earlier when I said that, depending on your attachment style, you tend to seek one overarching, important thing in your relationships overall? For anxious folks, you seek confirmation that your partner will not reject or abandon you. For avoidant folks, you desire maintaining independence. Simply put, anxious folks fear abandonment, while avoidant folks fear entrapment. Disorganized folks often fear entrapment at times and abandonment at other times (Levine and Heller 2010). How does this overarching need surface in relationships? Enter protest behaviors.

Protest behaviors are the things we do when our way of attaching, and our subsequent need for closeness (anxious) or distance (avoidance), is in danger (Benson 2023). Take the example of a woman who calls her partner only to get his voicemail. Anxious protest behavior might be calling his phone ten times or texting his friends asking where he is. Avoidant protest behavior might look like someone suggesting a break-up whenever they get into a fight with their partner. Say their partner got frustrated with something they did, and it's not the first time they've had that complaint. In their mind, they see themselves as a failure, and no longer wanting to disappoint their partner and be tasked with failing to change their behavior, they say, "Maybe we just shouldn't be together." The idea of needing to change who they are threatens their independence, and therefore they protest this feeling of entrapment by suggesting an end to their relationship.

Protest behaviors include demanding excessive reassurance, frequent nagging, acting distant or withdrawn, engaging in possessiveness, or doing things to make your partner jealous (Benson 2023). These behaviors are often a good place to identify what you may be doing that makes the interaction worse.

The Dance of the Anxious/Avoidant Relationship

This is where we get into the push/pull of relationships. You may have noticed that I outlined two examples, one anxiously attached person and one avoidantly attached person. Let's say those two people are dating each other, a likely occurrence as anxious and avoidant people are often attracted to each other. Anxious people often see avoidant folks as a worthwhile challenge toward obtaining the emotional closeness they so desire. Avoidant people are attracted to anxious folks, whose anxious behaviors further validate the avoidant person's needs for distance (Levine and Heller 2010). Here's an example of how these two attachment styles interact with one another.

> Kira, an anxiously attached woman, has a regular complaint that her partner, Marie, never lets her know when she is coming home, leading Kira to consider worst-case scenarios. Kira's father struggled with alcoholism when she was growing up and, as a child, she never knew when he would come home or what state he would be in. When Marie comes home hours after she says she will, it takes Kira back to being a scared child waiting for her dad to come home.
>
> Marie grew up in a very aloof and distant household. As a kid, she came and went as she pleased, and neither of her parents seemed to care about her whereabouts. Now, her independence is one of her favorite things about herself. When Kira gets angry at her for not texting, Marie sees it as an affront to her independence and immediately recoils, shutting down and going silent. The more Marie shuts down, the more Kira feels as though Marie is about to abandon her.
>
> Although Kira is unaware of this, her abandonment fear comes from her father leaving for days at a time, which he'd tell

her was because she had misbehaved. Marie shutting down reminds her of how her dad behaved right before he left, which sends her anxiety into hyperdrive. To make matters worse, Marie seeks distance when she's stressed out. When they get into a conflict, the way Marie has learned how to take care of herself is by going on long drives alone. Kira asks Marie where she's going and when she'll be back. Frustrated, Marie says that she doesn't know, viewing Kira's questions as stifling. The more Marie turns away, the more Kira pleads to get her to open up. She yells, cries, and threatens the relationship. These protest behaviors only push Marie further away. Marie protests by leaving on a long drive and turning her phone on silent. These series of interactions only create more distance, dissatisfaction, and frustration on both sides.

This push-pull dance is extremely common, one that is hard to stop and reset on your own, especially when one or both parties are unaware of what else is at play in terms of trauma and attachment. What started as a simple texting issue became a huge blowup, which is how fights often occur. Something small snowballs into something larger, tension builds, and then, all of a sudden, there are tears, hurt feelings, and a mountain of misunderstandings. It can be hard to know where to even begin to change these patterns but by building self-awareness around your own relationship patterns, including what *you* do that makes things feel stuck, you can start to unstick yourself.

EXERCISE: Self-Accountability

The last step of working *with* your attachment style is practicing self-accountability; that is, taking responsibility for the things you can

control—your behaviors and communication strategies. At http://www
.newharbinger.com/54384, you'll take a deeper look at your protest
behaviors. You'll ask yourself what you would need from yourself, your
partner, and others, and reflect on how you could get your attachment
needs met in a more productive way using communication, problem
solving, and self-soothing

Remember, anxious folks often need self-soothing strategies and
reassurance from partners, avoidant folks usually need to get space or
feel unconstrained. Disorganized folks might need both of those things
at different times.

This exercise will help you link your attachment style to the way
you show up in your relationships, build awareness, take accountability
around your protest behaviors, and brainstorm some new ways of
getting your relational needs met.

What Do We Do About It?

One thing to remember is that attachment styles are not pathologi-
cal—they simply *are*. Try not to judge yourself if you have one of the
insecure attachment styles. I get it—it would be really nice to have a
secure attachment style, but you're not destined to struggle in relationships if you don't. Try instead to see this as necessary information, almost like a guidebook not only to how you like to be loved but
also how problems will arise, as they will in any relationship. In fact,
understanding your attachment style and the attachment style of
your past, present, or future partner(s) puts you ahead of the curve.
Instead of seeing it as your fault or their fault when you get into a
conflict, now you have a road map that suggests the problem is
simply in the way you relate to one another.

Putting It All Together

I've thrown a lot of information at you. So far, you've learned:

- what type(s) of childhood wound you may be carrying into adulthood;

- what childhood relational trauma is and its different types;

- how childhood relational trauma impacts our adult relationships and repeats overtime;

- how trauma and attachment impact our stress responses and survival circuits;

- how attachment predicts our adult relationship patterns.

You've even gotten a sense of what attachment style you have and done some initial work around building awareness and accountability to use that knowledge to get your needs met in your relationships.

In the following chapters, we are going to take the knowledge you've gained and apply it to the real-life situations that are causing you stress, pain, misunderstanding, and dissatisfaction. We'll continue to build self-awareness, tend to your childhood wounds, and cultivate your ability to trust your authentic self and needs in order to gain the confidence to get what you need from yourself and your loved ones.

CHAPTER 3

Build Self-Awareness

Relationships often succeed or fail based on one key factor: communication. It's often both the problem and the solution (Lavner, Karney, and Bradbury 2016). Communication requires a healthy dose of self-awareness. We need to understand our own thoughts, feelings, capacities, and needs so we can communicate and respond to our partners in positive ways. Our caregivers didn't heal their own wounds and gain the necessary self-awareness. Unfortunately, we cannot change their subsequent behavior but we *can* change the way we respond to their behavior, as well as our responses to the behavior of our partners and loved ones. We do this through building self-awareness by practicing mindfulness (Benson 2023; Bassam 2013).

Mindful Awareness

When we are aware of our feelings, we can harness them into making choices that offer us support and deepen connection. I've said before that all feelings are valid. If you grew up suppressing or being ashamed of your feelings, you may believe the exact opposite. Depending on cultural and social messaging, you may have learned that crying was a dramatic bid for attention or that anger meant you were out of control. Consider instead that all of our *feelings* are valid, but our *behaviors* that result from our feelings are not always helpful, productive, or effective.

To build the relationships we deserve, we need to strengthen our relationships with ourselves first. We do this by recognizing how our feelings impact our thoughts and actions.

Let's look at an example:

Malika grew up feeling unseen and believing that no one cared about her, a belief that continued into adulthood. After a long day of work, she tells her husband, Jason, that she doesn't feel valued by her boss. Jason immediately starts to list some suggestions: "Well, why don't you bring it up to your boss? Have you tried to say it this way..."

"Just forget it!" she snaps, disappointed and dejected. Both of them retreat into silence, confused about what went wrong. Jason wonders, What did I do?

In essence, a communication breakdown occurred. Malika sought something from Jason, he tried but failed to provide what he thought she needed. Both of them shut down, feeling disconnected. Let's take a closer look at this scene with the childhood relational trauma added in.

When Malika opens up about work, she already feels vulnerable in sharing her frustration because her internal working model says she needs to handle her problems on her own.

When Jason cuts her off, it reminds her of feeling unseen in childhood, especially by her stepmother, even though she's not consciously aware she's comparing them. Her face gets hot, and she feels a mix of shame and anger.

She's thinking, Here we go again! My work problems are too much for him to handle. All he cares about is doing it his way. Does what I say even matter to him? Do I even matter?

But she doesn't say any of that. Instead, her fight mode engages, and she cuts him off and yells, "Just forget it!"

The picture I'm painting is common. Two people with good intentions, desiring connection but ending up further apart than before. So what is there to do about it?

Since patterns become stable over time, we start to prepare for what we already believe will happen. Jumping into problem solving may be the way Jason often responds to hearing about Malika's problems. Yet feeling unseen taps into a deep and hidden place within her, where her wounds of childhood live. The situation very quickly stops being about the present-day interaction and begins to symbolize a lot more: it encompasses how Malika sees herself, how she experiences Jason, and what she believes is possible in the relationship.

By now, your head might be spinning. You may be asking yourself, *If all this underlying meaning can exist in the span of a few minutes, how am I ever supposed to connect in the exact right way with anyone?* Thankfully, it is simpler than you may think. Back to self-awareness.

Consider that you, as the reader, already know more about Malika's internal world than she or Jason do. Say Malika felt nervous and frustrated about her day, and was eager to talk to her husband. When he started offering solutions, she felt a combination of anger and despair.

In this case, self-awareness would require Malika to recognize in real time that she is feeling those feelings. If she has developed a consistent mindfulness practice, she might even label them out loud to her husband at some point during their interaction: "I feel frustrated and sad when you jump to solutions." This may seem like no big deal; however, being aware of our moment-to-moment experience is often the difference between *feeling* our emotion and *acting* on our emotion. Mindful awareness creates a pause, giving us enough time and space to make a different choice—to communicate our feelings instead of exploding and yelling, "Just forget it!"

Here are some activities for you to try to begin to build your own self-awareness practice. Mindful self-awareness is a wonderful skill to practice every day. Some phone apps even have you log your mood at the same time every day, or you can log it when you feel a particularly big emotion. Get in the habit of noting how you feel at least once per day. You can even start to track your feelings over time and notice themes. For example, "Sunday scaries" identifies the experience many people share of feeling anxious right before the work week begins.

EXERCISE: Identifying Your Feelings

Close your eyes for a moment and consider the feelings that came up for you during the last argument you had with a loved one. If you can't think of one, you can reflect on how it felt to read about Malika and Jason's argument. If you are struggling to come up with feelings words, go to http://www.newharbinger.com/54384. There, you'll find a Feelings Wheel you can use as an aid.

Jot down three feelings that arise, using a piece of paper, a journal, or your phone. Make sure you jot down actual feelings words. Sometimes we mistake thoughts like "I felt like she wasn't listening to me" for feelings, when the feeling might actually be "frustration" or "disrespected."

EXERCISE: Body Mapping

Next, let's practice taking the feelings you listed and locating them in your body. Have you heard people say "I just had a gut feeling;" "I had a nervous feeling in the pit of my stomach;" and "I could feel the hairs stand up on the back of my neck"?

When you notice your body's physical sensations, you are building a connection between those sensations and the feelings you are experiencing. Building this mind-body connection is a very important part of practicing self-awareness, as our bodies are constantly giving us cues to how we are experiencing the world (Nummenmaa et al. 2014). When we are scared, we may feel a shiver down our spine. When we are grieving, we may feel a tightness pressing down on our chest or have the urge to gasp for air. When we are happy, we may feel a lightness or positive energy coursing through our body.

Have you ever been extremely stressed at work and then, just when you thought you couldn't feel any more overwhelmed, you also came down with a cold? That's the mind and body working together...against you. When we are feeling stress in our mind, our physical sensations are just a hop, skip, and jump away from showing that stress in our body.

Imagine the fight you thought about again. Think about what happened, what was said, and how it felt. Try and really place yourself back there. Slowly, with eyes closed and distractions minimal, see if you can pinpoint exactly where in your body you feel the feelings you listed above. If those feelings have subsided, label any new emotions that have arisen and see where you can locate those in your body.

If you're new to locating a specific feeling in your body, you may find it difficult. If that's the case, just see if you can notice anything at all happening in different areas of your body; for example, tightness or looseness, heaviness or lightness, hot or cold, pain or lack thereof.

For your convenience in using them repeatedly, this exercise and the one that follows are available for download at http://www.newhar binger.com/54384.

EXERCISE: Body Scan

If you're having trouble picking out any sensations, practice what's called a *body scan*. With eyes closed, turn your attention to one section of your body at a time, starting with your toes.

As you focus on one part of your body at a time, ask yourself: *What do I notice? Do I feel any sensations?* On a separate piece of paper, jot down any body sensations you notice. Then, move progressively upward, asking yourself the same questions about the soles of your feet, your ankles, your calves and shins, your knees, your thighs, your pelvis, your hips, your belly, and so on until you reach the crown of your head.

Reflect on what you noticed. There are no right or wrong answers here. The most important thing with body mapping is to exercise your self-awareness muscles. If your toes feel cold, that's great, you noticed. If your thighs feel tense, it's wonderful that you became aware. Congratulate yourself: you are actively grounding yourself in the present moment as you practice how you are feeling in your body *right here, right now.*

These two skills are crucial because they help us tap into the present moment. When we are triggered by a past wound or upset by what is happening in the present moment (or both), we tend to go very quickly into our minds to come up with explanations for why we feel the way we do, without knowing we are doing this. Sadness quickly becomes proof that no one cares about you. Jealousy quickly turns into a belief that you're not as handsome as the other guy at the party. When we identify our emotions and tap into our bodies, we are actively slowing the process of assigning an unhelpful narrative to our feelings.

Have you ever had a fight escalate so quickly that you thought, *How did we get here?* Or have you ever been mildly worried about something and then started thinking about the worst-case scenario and suddenly felt panicky? By identifying your emotion and placing it somewhere in your body, you are forcing yourself through a new process that got skipped when you weren't as aware. Now, you're effectively giving your brain space and time to catch up to the physical and emotional sensations you are experiencing. This small amount of space and time is crucial to making a different choice with your actions. In essence, you are emotionally de-escalating yourself. When we are tuned in to our present experience, we have more control around what comes next.

Impact Statements

If Malika and Jason came into my office, I would ask her, at that moment, to turn to her husband and communicate her feelings. This communication is called an *impact statement*. It is one of the cornerstones of effective communication. When I am communicating at my best with those in my personal life, I am using impact statements. When I get into conflicts that don't go well, it's usually because I have forgotten to start with "I feel…"

The basic formula of an impact statement is: "I feel [feelings word] when [describe the specific behavior your partner is exhibiting]."

This tool is important because, when we are feeling a difficult emotion, it's very easy to go straight to blaming the other person. Remember, all feelings are valid, so we are not trying to change the feeling; we're simply going to center the feeling first.

"You never listen to me!" we might say when we're upset. However, that is both an absolute statement (implying that we feel this 100 percent of the time) and an assumption about what has occurred (which will always be based on our own perception).

When you've experienced relational trauma, it's very easy to link your difficult feelings with your internal narrative that is also absolute: *no one cares about me*. Instead, Malika can complete the impact statement with only the facts of what actually occurred: "I felt sad and frustrated when I talked about how my day was and you immediately offered solutions."

Try it with a partner or another significant person in your life. Practice giving each other one impact statement that includes difficult emotions, like worry or sadness, and one impact statement that centers on emotions we look forward to, like happiness and excitement.

Make sure you are facing each other and minimizing distractions. Don't interrupt or respond to what the other person is saying. The topic you choose could be about anything: a conflictual topic or a more benign one, like what you are looking forward to doing this weekend.

Example: *I feel excited when I think about going away this weekend with you. I feel stressed when I remember that I have so much work to do when we are away.*

Impact statements may seem like an overly simplistic strategy. Believe me, I felt that way when I was starting out as a therapist. But I've seen firsthand how changing the communication strategies at the *beginning* of a fight, or even before the conflict starts, can have a hugely positive impact on the rest of the interaction. Shifting the beginning of an interaction by centering each person's feelings slowly but surely helps the relationship dynamic change.

Identifying Needs

As you might suspect, an impact statement alone is not going to solve a major rift in a relationship. That's where identifying needs comes in.

It's very easy to tell our partners what they do that upset us, but it's not particularly motivating. What if you told your partner what they could do to show up for you? Renowned couples therapist John Gottman calls this "helping our partners shine for us" (Gottman, Gottman, and DeClaire 2006). This is the difference between: "You never show up on time!" versus "It would be so helpful if you made it a priority to meet with me on time." Here, meeting you on time would be "shining for you."

The other thing you might have noticed about that example is how specific that need is. It's less helpful to say something like "I need you to show me respect," because what feels respectful to one person is vastly different than what feels respectful to someone else.

To ask for what you need, you have to *know* what you need. If this feels tough, you are not alone! It is incredibly common to struggle to know exactly what you need on a moment-to-moment basis. It's not as if we learn this in school. Additionally, if you experienced relational trauma that resulted in fawning or freezing, you've likely learned how to consider another person's needs while suppressing your own. If this is you, give yourself some grace. Your first step will be to consider that you *have* needs.

EXERCISE: Recognizing Individual Needs

This exercise, which is available at http://www.newharbinger.com /54384, combines self-awareness with identifying moment-to-moment needs. Block out twenty minutes of uninterrupted time on a day where you are not working, caring for someone else, or otherwise busy. Practicing mindfulness—that is, observing the thoughts that come into your mind without judging them—listen to what you want to do and then do it. If your body says, "I'm thirsty!" notice that internal message and then go pour yourself a glass of water. If you feel hungry, grab yourself a snack. If you feel lonely and like you want to text a friend, do that. If you want to take a bath, go for it. If you feel a certain emotion, write it down on a separate sheet of paper. If you have a thought, write that down too. Write down any thoughts you are having about this exercise in particular. If you get a strong urge to stretch, sing, cry, jump up and down, and burrow under your bed covers, do it all. Simply practice listening to yourself and your needs and desires and doing exactly what your inner voice says to do (within the confines of safety and reason) for twenty minutes.

This is a practice of mindful awareness. You are spending intentional time listening to your inner voice. This is the voice that says: *I'm hungry, I want to take a nap, I want to watch that show, I want to call my friend, I don't want to pick up that phone call.*

Relational trauma can make that inner voice hard to hear. If you are someone who has others depending on you, like children or ailing family members, you likely have become very skilled at ignoring your needs and wants while you attend to someone who requires your care. Or, if you learned how to appease others to stay safe, your internal voice that tells you what you need on a moment-to-moment basis may be very quiet or downright silent. This is a practice to come back to awareness of your internal cues that let you know what you need when you need it. This won't stop you from getting hijacked by your trauma but will help you begin to notice and eventually trust your inner voice that has always known what you needed, all along.

Later on, we will discuss our deeper core needs as well as how to separate those from our more surface wants. This exercise is getting you to build the muscle of mindfulness, the act of noticing where you are and what you need in the present moment.

For some this practice might be easy-peasy, and for others it may send you into a panic. Wherever you are is exactly right. Jot down some ideas about what came up for you when the twenty minutes have elapsed. What was easy about the practice? What was difficult? Did you learn anything about yourself? Did you struggle to hear what you needed? Were you conflicted about your needs? Do you know what you need but second-guess yourself? Maybe you wanted to text a friend but then thought, *Nah, they're probably busy.* Maybe you know what you need when you're by yourself but as soon as someone else is in the room, it becomes difficult for you to remember you still have needs.

EXERCISE: Specifying and Prioritizing Relational Needs

Now that you've practiced becoming aware of the fact that you *have* needs, let's see if we can focus on the deeper needs you have in your relationships.

Look at the list below and pick out a few needs that resonate immediately for you in your romantic relationships. Some of these might be overarching nonnegotiables, and some of these might arise only a couple of times throughout the course of your relationship. This exercise is almost like when we are searching for a new place to live—we have our absolute musts (needs) and our nice-to-haves (wants).

Use a piece of scrap paper (or download the chart at http://www .newharbinger.com/54384) to write down the needs that resonate with you under two columns: Needs and Wants. If there's a phrase that's almost right but not quite, write it in your own words by making it more specific to you. Humans are wonderful at knowing what we need; sometimes we just need to be reminded and heal the parts of us that continue to help us forget.

- To have my efforts acknowledged

- To connect spiritually/religiously

- To share my mental load

- To divide household chores and errands

- To share parenting responsibilities

- To have transparency and shared decision making about finances

- To engage in deep conversations

- To be complimented on my physical traits or personality traits, especially my _____

- To feel physically close to you especially when we _____

- To feel like we are both putting equal effort in as it relates to _____

- To have you initiate the next time we see each other

- To feel desired

- To go on dates

- To have you come up with a plan for our next date

- To have you ask about _____

- To have you put your phone away when we're talking

- To have you stand up for me when _____

- To share how I'm feeling during _____

- To know when I've done something that upsets you

- To do these activities together: _____

- To do these activities separately: _____

- To be held accountable for my mistakes in a kind way; for example, when you start by saying: _____

- To see evidence of change when you've done something that is hurting me, such as _____

- To feel empathized with when I talk about _____

- Add a need of your own:

- Add a need of your own:

What was hard about listing and categorizing your needs and wants? What was easy?

Now that you've done some work identifying individual and relational needs, we're going to consider how being triggered is related to getting our needs met both by ourselves and our loved ones. The next section is about building self-leadership, or our ability to feel and think, know what we're feeling and thinking, and then choose to communicate what we need from those around us. Self-leadership is the opposite of a loss of control; it's being your own best manager. You know how a great manager knows when to give directives, when to point out something that needs fixing, and when to give praise and understanding? That's what we're going to learn how to do for ourselves.

Identifying Your Triggers

The term "trigger" has become overused in popular media. You may wonder what the difference is between being triggered and having an emotional reaction. The key difference is that, when provoked by a stimulus, a trigger awakens past trauma that the person mentally relives in the present. An emotional reaction takes place only in the present moment.

For example, Jamie experienced psychological abuse as a child and now feels terrified after disappointing their partner. Without trauma, an emotional reaction may be Jamie feeling sad that they disappointed their partner. The intensity of the reaction is greater and the past is being relived only in the first example.

It can be incredibly difficult to give ourselves grace when we've been triggered. It's important to remember that we don't always have full control over our emotional reactions, though we can work toward having an impact over how we respond to the world around us. In fact, I often tell clients that the goal is not to never be triggered again, but instead to build awareness around when we tend to get triggered so we can be prepared to handle our big feelings and unhelpful thoughts.

If you are well versed at invalidating or being unkind to yourself, these next exercises may be difficult. In fact, you may have already bristled at what I've suggested you do thus far, thinking, *Okay, but aren't you just excusing bad behavior? Don't I need to be held accountable?* I've found there's real pushback when I ask people to practice self-kindness or compassion, for fear of letting ourselves off the hook or getting stuck in our feelings. Remember, a healthy level of self-critique is good; it's the frequency, intensity, and duration of our self-critique that makes it problematic. If you never say a kind word to yourself, you're not doing yourself any favors. You may believe that this harshness is *why* you're successful and functional; however, consider that your success may actually be *in spite of* this harshness.

Becoming emotionally triggered feels like having your body hijacked. It seemingly happens in a split second: a stimulus and then an immediate response. In actuality, there is a whole chain of associations and reactions that occurs within the moment of triggering.

When there's a triggering stimulus, the part of our brain that regulates our fight/flight/freeze/fawn response gets activated (Gass and Ansara 2015). When triggered, we're reliving past trauma by having an intense emotional reaction. We are immediately brought back into the past, and respond similarly to the way we responded at the time the trauma was actually occurring.

We can get triggered by any number of things—a phrase, a sound, a smell, a time of day, a season, or even a particular day of the year (Hopkin 2004). Have you ever felt overcome with sadness on the same date someone close to you died many years ago? This is an *anniversary reaction*, a common type of trigger for those who have experienced loss. Your body remembers the trauma that occurred on this exact day, and, subsequently, you may find yourself reliving intense memories and experiencing difficult emotions, even on the days leading up to the anniversary.

It is important to acknowledge how debilitating it can feel when we're triggered. It's even more important in our relationships because, when we are triggered, we act in outsized ways that may confuse our partner. Has your anger ever gone from 0 to 60 in two seconds when your partner used a particular tone with you? Chances are it wasn't just the tone that made you react that way. It may have been something from your past that got triggered. It's important for you to do the work to better understand what else is at play that causes a big reaction.

It is common for people to not know what they're feeling before they act on their emotions. If we are well versed in invalidating our emotions or suppressing our emotions, we may not even know what we are feeling when we are feeling it. With this in mind, we need to learn new ways to tend to our emotions. The first step is knowing what we're feeling. The best way to do this is to acknowledge that emotions have both a physical and mental component. With the body acting as our guide, we can start to learn *where* in our body we feel *which* emotion. Building self-awareness can help us learn what we're feeling in the moment in order to identify our triggers. You can refer back to the earlier body scan and mapping exercises for this.

EXERCISE: Getting to the Heart of Your Triggers

At http://www.newharbinger.com/54384, you'll find an exercise that asks you to think about a time when you were incredibly upset or angry (adapted from Gass and Ansara 2015). You'll choose an experience where you felt hijacked by your emotions, like you had no control over how you responded, and write down exactly what happened in a sentence or two. You'll recall the *facts*, not your *interpretation* of what happened.

Next, like riding on an elevator, you'll keep going down level after level to get to the heart of what happened. The top floor is your first reaction to the triggering event.

The third floor is usually a deeper, more vulnerable feeling that is linked to how you acted.

The second floor may lead to even deeper, less accessible, more vulnerable feelings.

The basement is usually our childhood wound, which is so sensitive, painful, and threatening that we will do anything to avoid confronting it. The childhood wound drives the whole triggering pattern.

After you've completed this exercise, notice the difference between what happened and the way you *interpreted* what happened based on your wounds. This illustrates the richness of our internal world. There is a difference between what *factually* occurs and the way we *perceive* it—both are important, but separating the two is imperative so that we can acknowledge that our perception of the problem (and our loved one's perception of the problem) is part of what gets us stuck.

EXERCISE: Tracing Back Our Triggers

Once we have identified each floor on the elevator shaft leading to the core wound, let's examine how and when this wound resurfaces throughout our life in other contexts and relationships. Trace it back to your earliest memory of having felt this way, looking for what appears to be the origin of this pattern (Gass and Ansara 2015). Taking your time to respond in detail, use the common trigger that got activated to answer these questions; you can download them at http://www. newharbinger.com/54384:

When have you felt this way before? Think of other situations, contexts, and relationships that have brought up these feelings and core wounds.

What is the earliest memory you have of feeling this way? Who was involved?

What else triggers this feeling? List everything you can think of. It may be specific triggers like sounds, smells, locations, specific social interactions, phrases, or particular questions. See if you can connect any of your physical triggers to your emotional ones. For example, maybe a loud clanging sound makes you feel unsafe or someone interrupting you makes you feel like you aren't valued.

EXERCISE: Tending to Triggers

Now that you have identified some of your specific triggers and considered where they came from, it's time to practice what to do *while* you are triggered. We are going to build on body mapping and scanning by connecting it to your triggers.

Think about the time you were triggered that you wrote about earlier, or use this exercise during a moment when you are currently triggered.

1. *Notice:* Take one deep breath in and out. Notice your surroundings, using your five senses to orient your body in the present. Notice your feet on the ground or your seat in the chair. Take note of your posture. Are you standing

upright or slouching? Take note of the temperature on your skin. Are you hot or cold? Do you smell or taste anything?

2. *Ground:* Close your eyes and think back to a time when you felt very safe. Where were you and what were you doing? Visualize that moment.

3. *Identify:* See if you can pinpoint the exact moment when your body started to feel distress.

4. *Replay:* See if you can rewind the tape, slowly playing back how you went from calm and relaxed to stressed and triggered. On a separate piece of paper, jot down any details— people, conversations, objects, behaviors—that were part of your environment.

5. *Tune in:* Tune back in to your body and notice again any sensations you have—numbness, tingling, temperature, or tension.

6. *Heal:* Place your hands on the area of your body that is feeling the most activation. If you can't pinpoint an area, put your hands on your heart. Visualize that feeling as a colored shape and imagine it sitting in the space in your body that you are touching. Take three more deep breaths. Allow that shape to expand, giving it as much space as it needs. Let that feeling wash over you, and see if it starts to dissipate.

You can practice this six-step process before, during, or after a stressful situation. You can practice it anywhere, whenever you need. Just like meditation, coming back into your body to give yourself a moment of presence and safety has incredible benefits for your stress level, personal wellness, and relationship health.

What Gets in the Way of Communicating Our Needs in Relationships

In my practice, when I work on identifying and specifying needs, folks get stuck in a variety of ways. One common way is what I call the "they should already know" fallacy. Chances are, you may have already communicated a need to your partner that they are having trouble satisfying.

Let's say you need to have an equitable division of labor in your relationship. The way you specifically want to get this need met by your partner is by having them take out the trash before it overflows. If you've already expressed this need and it hasn't been satisfied, it can be extremely difficult to motivate yourself to ask for it again, and again, for fear of continually being rejected.

I hear you. We want to be heard above all, and, when we're not heard by those who matter to us, it's painful. In your childhood home, perhaps all of the household chores fell on your mother, which resulted in her having very little time for your emotional needs. It is important for you to break that cycle and have a partner who takes an equal share in the household chores. When they don't, it makes you feel disrespected and overwhelmed, and fear that those generational patterns are repeating.

With trauma, not having our needs met can take us to a very dark place where what has occurred matches up with the worst voice in our heads. If your partner doesn't put the toilet seat down, suddenly it means they don't care about you. If your partner has stopped complimenting your body, that means they think you're desirable only when you look a certain way. Not getting our needs met can quickly take us to wounded places. Rapidly, we stop being upset about the need being unmet and start being upset by what we've decided that unmet need *means.*

When we get carried away by our unhelpful narratives, we often feel resentment or are afraid to ask again for our needs to be met. If you have a fawn or freeze response, it may be downright terrifying to ask for a need, for fear of burdening someone. Perhaps you believe that your partner "should" know by now and you "shouldn't" have to continually say what you need. Perhaps you're right. It can be very frustrating to do the emotional labor required to show those we love how to show up for us. Yet, time and time again, I see the damaging result of not giving voice to needs: resentment builds and conflict gets deprioritized, until one small thing sets you off and an explosive fight ensues.

Instead, I urge you to get ahead of that fight response by being clear about what you need as often as possible—first to yourself, and then to those around you. You and I, over the course of these very pages, cannot control whether the other person will satisfy those needs, but we can work on the empowerment and satisfaction that comes from advocating for your needs, especially if you grew up to believe you weren't allowed to have any.

For those of you who have done this work and continue to come up short, don't worry. Later on we will cover what to do when you've communicated your needs and they continue to be unmet.

EXERCISE: Reframing

When we desire something from someone, it's human nature to frame it in the negative:

"You didn't take out the trash."

"You're always on your phone."

"You aren't listening to me."

"You always pick what we watch on Netflix."

"We never go out anymore."

When we frame our desires in a negative way, we run the risk of demotivating our partner. However, when you help someone shine for you, you are showing them exactly how you like to be loved, cared for, and tended to. This means noticing when they do the thing you are asking them to do and pointing out their success, not only pointing out when they fail to show up for you.

The statements you just read become:

"Thank you for taking out the trash today. It makes me feel like we're a team."

"I feel most valued when you put your phone away during a conversation."

"It makes me feel listened to when you follow up with questions after I share something."

"I'd really love to watch this new show with you this week as a way to spend quality time together."

"I would love to hang out this weekend at the park and have you plan what snacks we'll bring."

Suddenly, the person who cares about us has an exact road map to our needs instead of having to listen to our critique and then try and figure out exactly what we want. When someone else is playing a guessing game, they often come up short, and then we must deal with the added disappointment of being let down again. By communicating your specific need in a positive way, you cultivate a climate of teamwork and communicate to this person: I am invested and accountable to *helping* you show up for me.

Think of something your partner does that frustrates you and start by framing it in the positive: "It would be so helpful if you _____."

Make sure you are as specific as possible. Think about parenting a child. Telling them to behave versus specifically asking them to keep their hands to themselves are two totally different messages—one is general and open to misinterpretation, and the other has a better chance of setting your kid up for success. Of course, our relationships with our loved ones and partners are not the same as our relationships with our children—in the latter, there is a hierarchy at play. Nonetheless, specificity is important across all relationships.

Next, check for understanding. If the person you are doing this exercise with isn't clear, this is the time to ask follow-up questions.

Let's say you told your partner: "It would be so helpful if you listened to me vent about work and empathized with me."

Your partner may understand this; however, chances are there is always an opportunity to further understand. Think of all the ways this could go awry. How long should they listen to you vent? What does empathy sound like to you? If they have a suggestion, should they voice it? What if they are confused and don't understand what the problem is? Can they ask for clarification?

Don't stop communicating until you both have the same understanding of how you want things to move forward. Once you've done that, switch positions. Your partner will be the one asking you to shine for them and you will be the one asking clarification questions. We will cover this more in chapter 5 when we discuss active listening and relational empathy.

How did this go? Think about what felt good. What felt weird? If you're not used to communicating in this way, and, let's be honest, few people are, it can feel weirdly clinical and not natural. That's okay and totally common, but it's not natural because you may never have learned to communicate in this way.

Putting It All Together

Think of these practices as strengthening a muscle or learning a new skill. If you've ever run a race, that first training session may have felt completely brutal. Your legs weren't working the way you wanted them to, and you may have been thinking the whole time, *This feels uncomfortable. I can't wait to stop.* Yet, with time and more runs, you slowly but surely started to get used to the way your body felt. Distances that were completely out of reach were suddenly accessible.

The same goes for these skills—the more you practice self-awareness and communication, the easier they will feel. These skills are new tools that you are adding to your toolbox. Maybe you already had a toolbox and you're just adding some new shiny tools, or maybe you needed to completely throw out your old toolbox because the tools were faulty and no longer working. Wherever you are, knowing that you have a toolbox of your own is a huge step in responding differently to the world around you. Trauma tells us we have no toolbox, that the only information we need to respond to the world around us is the information from the past.

Now that you've done some work around identifying your needs and communicating them, we are going to get deeper into *why* you need what you need and what makes it hard to get what you need. These exercises will shed light on how we treat and talk to ourselves, because in order to build fulfilling relationships, we need to start with the relationship we have with ourselves.

CHAPTER 4

Validate Your
Internal World

Now that you have a basic set of tools for building self-awareness around your thoughts and feelings and communicating them to your partner, let's go a bit deeper into your internal world.

People in relationships often get frustratingly stuck, not because their problems are unsolvable but because of the way they *think* and *feel* about their problems, which make them seem insurmountable. In fact, when I assess a couple sitting in front of me, I ask myself:

- What makes *this* problem *feel* unsolvable for *this* couple?

- What makes *another* couple *not* struggle with this problem?

- To make this problem easy to solve, what would each person need to know, feel, or do differently?

These questions all tap into how complex our internal worlds are. Our internal world—the way we think and feel about ourselves and the world around us—includes messages from our culture, heritage, personality, trauma, wounds, mental state, upbringing, preferences, life experiences, values, dreams, and fears, among many other things. You, too, can reflect on these questions for your own relationship difficulties in order to uncover information about your own and your loved ones' internal worlds.

Over the next chapter, you're going to learn more about your internal world so you can better understand what's at play when you are relating to another person. The deeper we know ourselves, the more we can pinpoint exactly what we want and need in any given situation. This self-knowledge can empower us to satisfy our own desires, ask our partners for the type of love and care that matters most to us, and do the same for them. Sounds easy enough, right? I wish it were! Unfortunately, there are so many barriers at play making it difficult to listen to what we want and need, but it is possible.

Internalizing Unhelpful Messages

One major barrier to tapping into our truest selves is the way we were socialized, meaning the messages we've received from our society, community, and the media. No matter where you grew up, you likely have internalized very strong messages about the "right" way to think, feel, and behave. These messages become so ingrained that separating what *you* think, want, feel, and do versus what society wants you to think, want, feel, and do can be nearly impossible. Consider also that within every culture, each of us grow up within a family that also has their own thoughts and feelings about the way we should behave. Social workers are trained to adopt a person-in-environment viewpoint, seeing each individual as a product of their larger context that contains interlocking and overlapping communities and environments. That approach helps us consider that there are so many more ways to view a situation other than simply right and wrong. It is by understanding that we all have a lens we look through, like a unique pair of prescription glasses, that we begin to understand where our thoughts, feelings, and behaviors come from. You can learn to do the same for yourself.

For example, coming from an academic family that valued and had the privilege to access higher education, it was very clear early on in my childhood that pursuing a college degree was nonnegotiable. I was never asked by my family members, "Will you go to college?" Instead, I was asked, "Which college will you go to?" Messages like these, sometimes implied and sometimes explicit, occur constantly in our family of origin as well as in the larger world we interact with on a daily basis.

The ways in which we seek out and engage in relationships are also impacted by the messages we receive. Growing up during the peak of 1990s romantic comedies, I learned that relationships were mainly about finding that one perfect person and, once you did, you would live happily ever after. What came after, from Hollywood's perspective, was irrelevant, as that first onscreen kiss was often the end of the movie. You may be thinking, *Surely we can tell the difference between real life and a movie!* However, I work with folks all the time who are looking to find their one true love, questioning if the person that they're currently with is "the one." In these cases, it can be hard to parse out what someone truly and deeply wants versus what someone wants because society has deemed it so.

We often internalize the messages we receive and behave accordingly, whether we are conscious of these messages becoming internalized or not. Remember, these messages are subjective, cultural, and contextual. Sometimes they are helpful, motivating, and empowering. Other times, as is the case with childhood trauma, they can be unhelpful, disempowering, harsh, and/or abusive. Internalizing problematic messages about ourselves and our abilities is one way that childhood trauma impacts us as adults. When we add in other factors that often occur alongside trauma, such as depression and anxiety, you might imagine that many of us tell ourselves a lot of unhelpful things that impact the way we feel and subsequently the way we act. For example, an adult who was often told by their parents growing up that they could do anything they put their mind to might say to themselves as they practice the guitar, struggling to reach the right chords, *I won't give up until my fingers have calluses! I can do this!* On the other hand, someone who grew up being told by their parents that they would never amount to anything may make one mistake during practice and think to themselves, *See? I can't do anything right. I'm useless at this too. I might as well give up.* Same activity, two vastly different internal worlds drastically impacting the result.

In this chapter's exercises, you are going to learn what unhelpful messages are swirling around in your mind, explore where these messages came from, and link these messages to your behaviors that make you feel stuck and dissatisfied in relationships. Next you're going to learn how to tend to your thoughts and feelings in a new way by talking kindly to yourself, practice fulfilling long-neglected needs, and get curious around this same process for your partner.

Invalidating Your Internal World

Before you learn how to validate your internal world, we need to explore how you may currently be invalidating your thoughts and feelings. *Invalidation* looks like rejecting, dismissing, or undermining your feelings, experiences, wants, and needs. Invalidating is likely something you learned how to do in childhood, as tending to your emotions with respect, kindness, and compassion is a relatively new parenting phenomenon. Consider the childhood wounds you identified. If you grew up feeling deprioritized, unworthy, guilty, abandoned, and/or unsafe, it is very likely that you learned how to invalidate your feelings.

One way we invalidate ourselves is by believing that we are doing something wrong when we feel negative feelings. I cannot count the number of times I've witnessed folks shaming themselves for crying over a breakup that they believe they were supposed to be over by now. When they feel upset, their internal voice says, *You shouldn't be upset anymore! This is pathetic! Get over it already!*

As a case against validating one's emotions, a fear I hear often is: "If I feel my feelings, I may never move beyond them." In fact, the opposite is true. Studies have found that the more we invalidate our feelings, the less able we are to effectively manage and move past them (Schreiber and Veilleux 2022).

With that in mind, go to http://www.newharbinger.com/54384, where you'll find an exercise that asks you to think about a problem you are currently having and then reflect on how you may be invalidating your feelings related to that problem by telling yourself any of these messages:

- This isn't a big deal.

- I'm just being dramatic.

- I don't even really care about this.

- I'm being too sensitive.

- I don't have a reason to feel this way.

- I just need to get over it.

- Others have it so much worse.

- I'm sure I'm just overthinking it.

- I'm taking things too personally.

- I'm such an idiot for responding like this.

- I'm probably overreacting.

In this short exercise, we are taking a first step to acknowledge the potential invalidation at play that might be preventing you from solving your problem. If you are avoidantly attached (one of the independent, self-reliant types who have difficulty being vulnerable in relationships), this might be an especially important step, as you may be well versed at suppressing your feelings altogether. You might even be having trouble coming up with a problem as you work to come online to your emotions. For anxiously attached folks, you may be well versed at self-invalidation, having been told you're overreacting by others, which may be a trigger for your anxiety. Once we acknowledge our tendency to invalidate, only then can we tend to our problem. Author and psychiatrist Dr. Dan Siegel (2012) calls this practice "Name It to Tame It." When we acknowledge what we are doing and feeling that is making us feel stuck, it becomes much easier to move past our "stuckness."

EXERCISE: Identifying Your Self-Limiting Beliefs

Self-limiting beliefs are self-deprecating or invalidating thoughts or beliefs that hold you back from regulating your emotions around it, giving yourself compassion, or allowing yourself to grow. When we are aware of the most common limiting beliefs, we can learn how to identify them when they arise within us and notice how they impact our behavior. With this awareness, we can learn how to shift these beliefs and respond differently to them.

I want you to think about the problem you described in the last exercise and write down any self-limiting beliefs that you have related to this problem, or that jump out at you as something you've heard yourself say in general. You can do this at http://www.newharbinger .com/54384.

Here are some common self-limiting beliefs to help you get started:

- I'm not good enough.

- I'm too old [or insert the self-deprecating adjective you use most often].

- I don't have enough time.

- I'm not worth it.

- I am unlovable/unlikable.

- I don't know what I'm doing.

- I'll never be happy/satisfied.

- I can't get what I need from others.

- I'll never be one of the best, so what's the point?

- I'm too much/too sensitive/too needy.

Self-limiting beliefs aren't all bad. Remember our evolved stress responses that make us fight, flee, freeze, or fawn? Self-limiting beliefs partially come from the part of our brain that evolved to ward off danger, only now we've become smart enough to keep ourselves away from danger by limiting our full potential with our thoughts. These beliefs may also come from cultural and societal messaging as well as personality traits and mental health issues. Part of understanding and tending to our self-limiting beliefs is about thanking the part of us trying to keep us safe and protected from harm.

Our self-limiting beliefs are based on our deepest fears, known as *core fears*, which ultimately inform our behaviors that try to prevent these fears from coming to fruition (Pressman 2019). Self-limiting beliefs arise in response to core fears. If the self-limiting belief is the engine, then the core fear is the destination we keep circling back to. In fact, we often pile self-limiting beliefs on top of one another, all stemming from and reinforcing the danger of our core fear.

EXERCISE: Identifying Your Core Fears

Core fears are often at the root of our anxieties as adults (Pressman 2019). Understanding them better can unlock new paths toward healing. A core fear is our internal world's narrative that makes all of our struggles feel particularly dangerous based on what we are afraid of. It is an interpretation we create in childhood that helps us understand the threatening things that happen to us. Say you get broken up with, and you experience this breakup as confirmation that your core fear is true: no one will ever love you. This core fear being activated makes the breakup feel not only painful but also dangerous and despairing.

Remember our childhood wounds? Our fear is what we are afraid of happening based on how we were wounded back then. If we were abandoned, we now fear more abandonment. If we didn't feel like we belonged, we now fear rejection. If we grew up believing love was conditional, we fear making mistakes and, ultimately, losing love. If we felt unsafe, we fear experiencing that same lack of safety again. If we grew up feeling guilt, we fear making others feel bad.

Our fears are a subjective interpretation that we make in childhood to characterize *how* we feel threatened by life's hardships. When we understand what we are most afraid of, we can recognize when these fears are coming into play and link our subsequent self-limiting beliefs and eventual behaviors together. A self-limiting belief that says *I'm too needy* touches on my core fear that *I will always be alone* because of it. Instead of reacting from a place of fear, we can use self-awareness to respond mindfully and intentionally, giving ourselves what we need or getting what we need from our loved ones. This might look like me challenging my self-limiting beliefs by saying "My partner did not have the capacity to give me what I needed, but it doesn't mean I'm needy. There are people out there who can meet my needs."

Common core fears include:

- abandonment or loss of love;

- loss of identity;

- loss of meaning;

- loss of purpose or expression;

- sickness or pain;

- loss of life.

Let's say Samar's core fear is abandonment by loved ones, due to his father suddenly dying when Samar was nine. Now when Samar has an issue, he thinks, *No one cares about me.* Because of this self-limiting belief, Samar is hyperindependent. He won't reach out to others when he has a problem because he tells himself, *I have to solve my problems by myself,* another self-limiting belief. He solves the problem by himself with no one in his community being aware of this, thereby confirming his self-limiting belief.

Our self-limiting beliefs spawn behaviors that create self-fulfilling prophecies, making our core fears more real and legitimate. When Samar asks no one for support, no one shows up, thereby making Samar's core fear that much more likely to occur.

Review the core fears above. Now, think about your problem from the last exercise. At http://www.newharbinger.com/54384, we're going to discover one of your core fears related to the problem you chose. Below where you wrote your self-limiting beliefs, you'll write down the answers to these questions. Make sure you write your answers in short and clear phrases.

Why is this problem upsetting to you?

What are you afraid would happen?

What are you afraid you would miss or lose?

Each question should push you one level deeper toward accessing what you are ultimately afraid of, or your core fear. If you are struggling to answer one of the questions, skip that question and try the next one. Use the list of core fears as a guide to see which of your answers most closely resemble those outlined. If you are still not reaching a core fear, keep asking yourself, *And what are you afraid of then?* until you arrive at a core fear.

Many of us have multiple core fears. Don't get too hung up on choosing the "right" one. The point of this exercise is to peel back the layers of our internal world so we can tap into what we're most afraid of and eventually see how our behaviors are informed by our fears and self-limiting beliefs. This deep self-knowledge will help us explain to our loved ones what matters most to us and allow us to get what we need.

Connecting Present Perceptions with Past Experiences

When I hear someone say something invalidating to themselves, like "I'm probably just overreacting," I sometimes ask, "Whose voice is that?" The voices in our head often sound eerily similar to the voices of those who raised us. Think about it: have you ever heard yourself say a phrase your parents used to say to you, and cringed, having sworn you would never utter those words yourself? Having control over our internal world is tricky as we can't always predict what's going on in there, and we wonder, *Is that me or is that my trauma?*

It's important to understand what messages we *truly* believe versus what messages we *internalized* from an early age, messages that got piled up on top of our true selves, burying our gut instincts and authentic ways of being. You have already started to think about how your childhood wounds have impacted the way you think about yourself. Now, let's go one step further.

EXERCISE: Connecting Your Past to Your Present

Choose the phrase you used to invalidate yourself or the self-limiting belief that resonated with you the most. Using a separate piece of paper or downloading this exercise at http://www.newharbinger.com/54384, write down your answers to these questions:

- Where does that belief come from?

- Does that phrase feel familiar? How?

- When did you first feel that way about yourself?

- Did anyone else you grew up with feel this way or similarly about you? About themselves?

- What were the messages you received about this feeling or experience growing up?

- How would your caregivers have handled the problem you're having?

- Can you think of an experience during your upbringing that relates to this problem?

Next, think about your core fear to answer these questions:

- Where did this fear come from?

- What childhood wound feels related?

- How does this fear relate to fears you grew up with?

- When is the first time you remember feeling this fear?

- Do you know anyone else with this fear?

- Do you know anyone else with the opposite of this fear?

- When were you most afraid of this fear actually happening?

During these exercises, you may have just scratched the surface of learning more about your internal world, or you may be fully down a rabbit hole connecting your present to your past. Wherever you are is where you need to be.

These exercises can be done alone or alongside deeper therapeutic work. Whatever your journey is, this is a good first start into making some connections about how and why you are who you are. If you are starting to make connections between your ways of thinking and how you were raised, you are on the right track. If you are starting to connect how your daily problems connect to what you're most afraid of, you are doing a wonderful job of learning more about your internal world, how it works, and what you will need to give yourself to tend to your feelings.

As you continue to practice validating your internal world, practice mindfulness the next time an issue arises. Any time you notice yourself invalidating your feelings, practice reminding yourself in the moment, silently repeating to yourself: *What I feel matters*. Notice how that impacts what you decide to do about this issue.

EXERCISE: Connecting Thoughts and Feelings to Behaviors

One of the best ways to build emotional intelligence is to understand how our thoughts (like our self-limiting beliefs and invalidating messages) and feelings (including our core fears and how we feel following our self-limiting beliefs) impact our behaviors, overall and in the moment. This understanding is the next step of learning about the vastness of our internal world. It's the difference between going from 0 to 60 when our partner says something that hurts our feelings, and knowing, in the moment or after the fact, that we reacted with anger because they touched on a deep insecurity that we know is there, which made us want to spend the rest of the day giving them one-word answers.

It's also important to note that our thoughts and emotions impact our behaviors, which also impact the thoughts, emotions, and behaviors of others. Think about how road rage happens. The entire interaction between two drivers may happen in a split second but when you slow the interaction down, what's happening is:

Someone cuts us off on the highway driving 90 mph (behavior) → We feel scared and angry (feeling) → We think, *Where did that person come from?* (thought) → We slam on our brakes (behavior) → thinking, *How dare they?* (thought) → We throw up our hands and curse them (behavior).

In the last few exercises we talked a lot about thoughts. Let's now connect some feelings to our thoughts. After that, we'll connect to how those thoughts and feelings drive us to behave in certain ways. Understanding the relationship between our thoughts, feelings, and behaviors is instrumental in understanding and healing our childhood wounds. They give us a map to follow how we think, feel, and behave, based on the pain we carry. We're going to use our core fears, invalidating messages, and self-limiting beliefs in this exercise because these are where many of our childhood wounds live.

Here are two examples of how childhood wounds show up in our thoughts and behaviors:

Guilt Wound

Situation: My friend wants to hang out but I'm tired.

Feeling(s): guilt, worry

Fear: disappointing others could lead to a loss of friendship (or loss of love)

Self-limiting belief: "Saying no is selfish."

Invalidation: "If I were a good friend, I'd say yes."

Behavior: saying yes and hanging out

Abandonment Wound

Situation: My partner has been silent all morning.

Feeling(s): worry, fear

Fear: abandonment and rejection

Self-limiting belief: "He's probably mad at me. What can I do to make it better?"

Invalidation: "I'm probably just overreacting."

Behavior: asking ten times if he's mad at me

At http://www.newharbinger.com/54384, you can download these questions about your feelings and thoughts, as well as the ones below about behaviors. You'll start by describing a tough time you had in the past week interacting with a partner or loved one.

Describe the situation.

What did you feel about the situation?

What did you think about the situation?

What did you think about yourself regarding the situation?

What were you most afraid of?

What wound got triggered?

Next, you'll think about how you acted in this situation. Did you shut down and remain silent? Did you start to play games and test your partner's love and affection for you? Attack the person nearest to you with your words? Panic and start distracting yourself by scrolling? Pretend nothing is wrong but find passive-aggressive ways to bring it up later? Stay in bed and binge-watch TV? Identifying your behaviors can be hard in the beginning because you may have never connected your actions to your thoughts and feelings.

You'll end this exercise by assessing what you do across a variety of situations. You may be saying, *How should I know? It depends on the situation!* In this case, I invite you to consider that we all act in patterns of behavior. Many people who grew up feeling unsafe find it difficult to let their guard down and get close to another person. If that's you, what does that look like for you? Others need constant reassurance that they won't be abandoned. What does that look like for you?

Tip #1: It's hard to be an objective observer as it relates to what we do. Our loved ones often have a good idea of how we behave when we're feeling certain emotions. Ask someone close to you: "What do I usually do when you've hurt my feelings?"

Tip #2: If you get stuck thinking about your behaviors, revisit the behaviors outlined in chapter 2's stress response and attachment section. When feeling a big emotion, do you have a tendency to fight, flee, freeze, or fawn? What about your protest behaviors? What do you do when you're not getting what you need?

You can download these questions at http://www.newharbinger .com/54384 or fill in your answers on a separate sheet of paper:

When I feel _____ and think _____, I tend to _____.

When I feel _____ and think _____, I tend to _____.

When I feel _____ and think _____, I tend to _____.

Connecting our thoughts and feelings to our behaviors is imperative in our relationships. When we know how our thoughts and feelings guide us to act in certain ways we can begin to notice patterns and reflect on how our patterns impact our relationships. With this new understanding, we can become skilled at tending to our emotions in different ways, shifting our unhelpful thoughts and subsequently changing our problematic behaviors that create conflict, dissatisfaction, and disconnection.

EXERCISE: Practicing Self-Affirmation

Rip up a piece of scrap paper into long, thin strips. On each strip, write one of the following affirmations and tape or place the strips in places you often look—your bathroom mirror, your refrigerator, your day planner, your bedside table. Feel free to write your own affirmations in your own words that would help you validate your internal world, emotions, or thoughts.

- There is nothing wrong with emotions.

- My feelings are not facts.

- We all have emotions.

- I am more than my feelings.

- I am more than what I feel at this exact moment.

- What I feel is different than how I act.

- I cannot choose how I feel, but I can choose how I act.

See what happens over the next week as you pay more attention to affirming your emotions throughout the day. Using your journal, jot down any ideas, experiences, or notes you have related to how these affirmations impacted your thoughts, feelings, and behaviors during the week.

EXERCISE: Moving from Self-Invalidation to Self-Affirmation

One of the hardest things about validation and self-compassion is that many of us have no idea how to talk more kindly to ourselves. Remember that list of invalidating phrases that are the first barrier to keeping you stuck? The ones that tell you that you shouldn't be feeling what you are feeling?

The chart below, which you can download at http://www.newhar binger.com/54384, provides two examples of self-affirmations that can replace self-invalidating statements. After reading the examples, you'll continue on to complete the chart.

It is way easier for us to validate someone we care about than it is to do it for ourselves. If you get stuck, imagine your best friend is saying the invalidating statement, and imagine what you would say to them to affirm them.

Self-Invalidation	Self-Affirmation
I'm fine.	It's okay to not always be fine.
This isn't a big deal.	This may not be huge in the grand scheme of things, and I'm still entitled to my feelings.
I don't even really care about this.	
I think I'm just too sensitive sometimes.	
I don't have a reason to feel this way.	
I just need to get over it.	
Others have it so much worse.	
I shouldn't feel like this.	
I'm such an idiot for responding like this.	
I'm probably overreacting.	

This week, challenge yourself to see if you can hear the next time you tell yourself something invalidating. See what happens when you challenge your self-invalidation with one of the self-affirming messages you came up with. Notice how it changes what you do and feel next.

EXERCISE: Thanking Your Safety Mechanism

Think of a situation that is currently bringing you stress. Look back at chapter 4, and pick the self-limiting beliefs that resonated the most with you. At http://www.newharbinger.com/54384, you'll find a chart that asks you to write your five most common self-limiting beliefs; acknowledge or thank the part of that belief that is trying to keep you safe; add an impact statement that describes how you feel about the situation; and end with a message to yourself that is positive, kind, nurturing, or caring. Make sure that your impact statement is not an *interpretation* of the situation, like a self-limiting belief, but a statement that describes how you *feel* about the situation. If you are stuck for positive self-talk, think about what you would say to a friend who was in distress. I've put an example below for reference.

Self-Limiting Belief	The Part Trying to Keep You Safe	More Accurate Impact Statement	Positive Self-Talk
I'm not good enough.	When I tell myself this, I am trying to protect myself from rejection.	I feel afraid of failing.	Whatever happens, I will be able to handle it.

Practicing Self-Compassion

The final step of validating your internal world requires you to practice self-compassion. Self-compassion is the perfect antidote to the invalidation or mistreatment you've experienced. It is also a powerful way to undo the impacts of your relational trauma (Germer and Neff 2015). We will never be able to change the horrible things that happened in the past, but we can change the way we view our present through the way we talk to ourselves, which, over time, will change the way we show up in the future. The kinder you are to yourself, the easier it is to be kinder to others, especially our partners. The meaner you are to yourself, the harder it is to be kind to others because of how quickly denying, judging, and mistreating ourselves erodes our ability to give to another. This phenomenon is called *compassion fatigue*. Being self-compassionate is an actual professional strategy used by therapists because when we are emotionally depleted it is near impossible to provide the compassion, understanding, acceptance, and empathy required for our clients.

With that in mind, let's give the steps of self-compassion a try:

1. Think about a recent mistake you made that impacted someone close to you.

2. Next, *pinpoint the emotions* you feel (or did feel) about that mistake. This step is important because it requires us to be mindful about our feelings in the moment. We can't practice self-compassion if we don't know what we're feeling when we're feeling it.

3. *Normalize this feeling* by connecting it to having a human experience. This step reminds us that we are not alone or unique in our suffering. Say something to yourself like, *What I am feeling is human. Many people make mistakes, and when we make mistakes, it's painful and embarrassing.*

4. *Give yourself what you need.* This may be the most difficult step because we don't always know what we need.
   One thing you may need is to be nurtured. Just as we did
   a few exercises ago, pretend you are your own best friend.
   What would you say to your best friend if they made the
   same mistake? Or think about what you may have
   needed as a child. Maybe that was a big hug, or to cry, or
   to dance with reckless abandon, or to take a nap. Giving
   yourself what you need is the first step toward healing
   that inner child who didn't get the specific nurturing
   you were looking for. Now, as adults, we are able to give
   that to ourselves and heal the parts of us that went
   without all those years ago. Maybe you need to ask your
   partner for something or communicate to them how you
   are feeling. Refer back to the exercise of identifying your
   needs in chapter 3 if you need some ideas.

Whenever you are faced with an issue or a big feeling, try using
the steps of self-compassion as a strategy to move past self-validation,
give yourself grace and compassion, and tap into what you need.

Exercise: Writing a Letter to Your Inner Child

Whether or not we have experienced childhood relational trauma, we
grow into adults who keep parts of our childlike selves inside of us,
parts that get triggered every once in a while. One of the best ways to
build self-awareness, emotional intelligence, and resiliency as an adult
is to acknowledge our inner child and tend to them when needed
(Sjöblom et al. 2016).

Think about the hardest year or season of your childhood. How old
were you? Using a separate piece of paper, write a letter to yourself at
that age. What would you want this child to know? What could you say
to make them feel seen, loved, and nurtured for exactly who they are?

What do you wish they had been given back then? You can give it to them now, through this letter. Give them the knowledge and wisdom you have from the future that would be helpful for them to know about—tell them about your successes, triumphs, and lessons learned. Give them hope and guidance.

Tip: If you are having trouble accessing your childhood feelings and experiences, look at some pictures, memory tokens, or videos from your childhood. You can also engage in activities you used to do as a kid—for example, drawing, singing, playing a certain sport. This can help take you back to that time, eliciting a better sense of what it was like to be that kid then. Be aware that this may bring up painful feelings. Take care of yourself, and use the grounding exercises from chapter 3 if you find yourself particularly triggered or emotionally activated.

Keep in mind that talking to your childhood self with love and compassion is not so different from talking to yourself kindly as an adult. In fact, look over your letter and underline any phrases that would be helpful to tell yourself as you move through life's current difficulties. If you memorize these statements, they can serve as mantras, or positive statements you say to yourself for affirmation or motivation, that you repeat to yourself, silently or aloud, when you need it. I often tell clients to write their mantras on Post-It notes and stick them in places they'll see on a daily basis. I have one on my laptop right now as I write this. It says, "You can do this." I even use positive mantras as passwords for many of my computer logins.

Doing inner-child work is similar to grief work. It can bring up feelings of sadness, despair, and even anger around what we didn't receive as children. Allow yourself to grieve. This is very common and totally natural. Grieving may make you feel guilty or ashamed—it may make you feel bad for the thoughts you are having about your childhood and caregivers. I invite you to consider that you can hold two concepts at once: frustration and sadness at what you didn't receive in childhood *and* understanding and compassion at your caregivers who may have done the best they could with what they had.

Building Self-Worth and Self-Esteem

So much of healing our childhood wounds is about getting back to who we were destined to be before trauma was layered on top of our truest selves. Inner-child healing can bring us back to our truest selves, where we can begin the work of building our self-worth and self-esteem from our unique and special gifts.

One of the biggest issues I come across is when people don't believe, deep down, that they deserve love and care; that is, they lack self-worth. This is the difference between self-esteem and self-worth. Self-esteem is the positive feelings we get from our abilities and achievements; self-worth is our belief that we inherently deserve love, care, and respect *regardless* of our abilities. Which one do you struggle with?

How you talk to yourself in your own mind reflects how you feel and think about yourself. At http://www.newharbinger.com/54384, you'll find an exercise that asks you to write down all the thoughts you have over the course of a few hours. You'll then reread what you've written and ask yourself:

- How critical are you of yourself?

- How often do you think unkind or judgmental things about yourself?

- How often do you think unkind or judgmental things about others?

- Do you believe you deserve respect and care?

- Do you believe others do?

- How would you feel if your loved one talked about you the way you do?

You'll cross out any thought that is particularly unkind, untrue, critical, or unhelpful, and replace it with a kinder, more accurate, more productive, or more helpful statement. If you catch yourself thinking these thoughts about yourself (and others) over the next few days, replace them with a kinder, more helpful voice.

Getting Curious About Your Partner's Internal World

This chapter has focused a lot on understanding and tending to our own internal world; however, our loved ones have internal worlds that are just as rich as ours. You can imagine how complex and complicated conflicts actually are when we consider that two people's internal worlds are learning to work together, often bumping up against each other and resulting in disconnection, misunderstanding, and frustrating feelings of stuckness.

Although you are not responsible for your partner's emotions and behaviors, you do have an impact and influence over them. If you grew up in an enmeshed family or have an anxious attachment style, this may be very difficult to believe, as enmeshment is marked by growing up to believe that you are, in fact, responsible for your family members' emotions. If you grew up in a distant and rigid family or have an avoidant attachment, you may believe the exact opposite, underestimating just how much your behaviors and emotions impact your partner and loved ones. In this way, striking that perfect balance of believing you have *influence* over your partner but not total *control* may be difficult to embody.

Consider all the work we just did on building awareness and tending to your internal world. Imagine that your partner has the exact same stuff swirling around for them, with anywhere from little self-awareness of all the moving pieces to a high level of understanding.

Imagine they react intensely to something you say and you sense that they have been triggered. Previously, without this new level of

97

awareness, you may have reacted strongly to their strong reaction. This pattern happens all the time in fights. In the same way the road-rage incident happened over the course of a few seconds, our worst fights with partners are often quick—tension builds, they react, we react, they react, and, having reached a boiling point, there's an explosion followed by an extended period of silence or distance before coming back together to repair or sweeping it under the rug for the next time.

The way to manage emotional reactivity is to slow things down, which requires you to be present in your body. Mindful presence, as you've seen, requires internal self-work on both sides. However, it is possible for one person to bring the other person along in that process through curiosity, empathy, and self-regulation.

EXERCISE: Practicing Curiosity During Conflict

Without self-awareness and curiosity, this is what a fight pattern often looks like:

Partner gets triggered and attacks → You get defensive → They get defensive → Fight escalates

In order to stop the pattern, we have to do something differently:

1. Instead of getting defensive back, take two deep breaths. Make sure your exhale lasts longer than your inhale, stimulating your *vagus nerve*, the part of your nervous system responsible for calming you down.

2. Notice that your partner is activated and ask with curiosity: "What's happening for you right now?" Depending on their level of self-awareness and emotional reactivity, they may or may not be able to answer. Again, this is largely their work, especially if you are able to ask this curious question with a calm tone and empathy.

3. If they cannot respond effectively, ask them if they want to take a five-minute break to calm down and self-regulate. During the break, do something that pulls your focus away from the conflict.

4. After the break, ask them about what was going on for them. Come from a place of curiosity, delving into their experience. This exercise is purely to help increase under-standing of your partner's triggers, so resist the urge to defend or explain your side. This can restart the conflict.

5. Ask them what they need from you. Sometimes, when we are triggered, the best thing is for a loved one to put their hand on our shoulder, give us a hug, or tell us it's going to be okay and that we're safe.

Putting It All Together

These exercises have involved acknowledging and honoring the vastness of your and your partners' inner worlds in order to get and give the love you both deserve. You've acknowledged that you've internalized unhelpful messages and used those messages to invalidate your genuine thoughts, feelings, and needs. You've pinpointed which self-limiting beliefs are holding you back and considered what you're most afraid of. You've worked to understand the context of these fears as it relates to your past and how it shows up in your present. You've even connected how these thoughts and feelings impact your behaviors to this day. You've taken all this information about how your internal world works and started to practice self-affirmations, self-compassion, and inner child healing. You've gotten curious about your partner's internal world and how it shows up in your relationships in order to better navigate conflicts. In the next chapter, we will build on this by practicing different ways to com-municate with your partner and loved ones.

CHAPTER 5

Communicate Effectively

In the last chapter, we were beginning to get curious about our partner's internal world during a conflict. Now, we are going to focus on using your knowledge of your internal world to communicate differently with loved ones. After all, this book isn't just about healing your childhood relational trauma, it's also about deepening connection to get and give the love you deserve.

You've learned more about where your wounds come from and how they surface in your daily life. You've built self-awareness around knowing what you do when things get tough. This self-awareness can bring you some predictability around knowing what you do, which can give you clues about what you need during those tough times. Self-awareness can help you see hard times in a slightly different way, instead of getting stuck in shame or despair. There is a major difference between saying to yourself *This is unfair and so I'm going to start a fight with my partner* versus *The story I'm telling myself is that this is unfair, so I'm going to take some time to figure out what about it feels unfair before I respond to my partner.*

We've done the work of better understanding ourselves; now we need to help our loved ones better understand us so they can give us what we need. In order to do that, we first need to be intentional about how and when we communicate.

Knowing When to Speak Up

Do you ever avoid bringing up hurt feelings or unmet needs because you don't want to start a fight? After a long day of work, school, or taking care of kids, the last thing many of us feel like doing is leaning into conflict with our loved ones, especially when we run the risk of it not going well.

Healing trauma requires building self-trust that comes from counting on yourself to be able to bring up your feelings and needs when it feels right to you and at a time that your loved one can receive it. So many people wait until their boiling point because urgency acts as the ultimate motivator when we can't hold it in any longer. However, our boiling point is the least productive time to talk vulnerably about our feelings and needs. And yet, unfortunately, it is often the time we feel bravest about speaking our minds.

Think about something important you have been meaning to talk to your loved one or partner about. Maybe you got your feelings hurt, maybe you've been meaning to enforce a boundary or give some feedback that makes you feel nervous. How can you tell if it's the right time to bring it up?

Consider that there are some relationships where it *never* feels like the right time to speak up because the other person always responds defensively, aggressively, or in an otherwise negative way. In these scenarios, I recommend communicating about this pattern specifically—"I've noticed that when I bring up a negative emotion you start yelling"—and seeking additional support from a therapist if you continually hit roadblocks. It is important in our intimate relationships to feel safe enough to bring up hard things. Extra support will be necessary if you constantly feel attacked, shut down, or minimized when you broach a difficult topic.

Responding yes or no to these questions will help you determine if now is the right time to speak up.

Will this person be able to listen to me fully?

Consider: What is going on for them right now? Do you notice any clues that they may not have the capacity to show up for you? Have they been particularly irritable today? Do they seem to be in the middle of an important project?

Am I currently emotionally calm?

Consider: Being in a good state of mind is imperative. If you don't feel calm, ask yourself what you would need to do to get into a better state of mind. For example, to center myself, I used to meditate right before a weekly meeting I dreaded.

Do I know why I feel upset or frustrated?

Consider: It is important to preemptively reflect specifically on why you feel the way you do so you can communicate clearly to your loved one. Think about what you want to say in advance.

Would this conversation be better suited for a different time?

Consider: Is there something you need to do before you speak up that would support the process? How much time do you have to have this conversation? Are you setting both yourself and the other person up for success based on the current situation?

Have I identified ways of resolving this issue?

Consider: Do you have some ideas about what you need moving forward? This is a great time to refer back to the list of needs in chapter 3 and do some thinking on how you might like to solve this problem by getting a need met. Maybe you need acknowledgment, an apology, an opportunity to problem solve proactively, space apart, time together, or a specific behavior from the other person.

Is it a good time?

Consider the environment, including your mood. Is it right before you're about to go to bed? Have you had a couple of glasses of wine? Are you already feeling depleted? Angry? Resentful?

If you said no to one or more of these questions, it may not be the right time to speak up. Hold off for a better time where you can answer yes to all of these questions. The next time you want to share something important, ask yourself these questions first.

Sharing Your Wounds with Your Loved Ones

Let's imagine that it *is* the right time to bring something up to your loved one. In the last chapter, we identified some of the unhelpful parts of our inner world, like our self-limiting beliefs, invalidations, and core fears. We learned how to center our feelings in our communication. Now let's put those pieces together and practice how we can describe our wounds during a conflict to give our loved one a deeper insight into who we are, how we work, and what we ultimately need. First, here's an example.

> *Jayden has been dating Lani for ten months, and everything has gone relatively smoothly. Lani has started a new graduate program and suddenly has a lot less free time than she used to. Although she had let Jayden know that this would happen, Jayden is worried that Lani is no longer as interested in their relationship as she used to be. There's been less texting throughout the day, and when Lani does text, it's less flirty than it used to be. Most of the communication has switched to planning logistics.*

Jayden is bummed that the texting, one of the things she loved the most at the beginning of their relationship, has gotten less regular. She worries that this is the beginning of the end, and she has begun to play the very games she swore she wouldn't when they first started texting. Jayden now waits longer to respond to Lani's text to see if that makes Lani more eager to communicate. Jayden also waits for Lani to make plans for the weekend, when before, she wouldn't have been shy about asking Lani out.

Jayden wonders if growing apart is simply what happens as more time elapses in a relationship. Is it fair for me to feel this way? she thinks. Lani did say things would change, so why is Jayden feeling so anxious and sad?

Jayden asks herself: Where have I felt these feelings before in my relationships? She has done some thinking around how her mom was very inconsistent in her affection. When Jayden's mom wasn't stressed with work, she was present. When she was stressed with work, her parenting became all about logistics, and Jayden couldn't get the emotional support she needed. It made Jayden feel like she couldn't truly sink into the times that her mom was available, for fear of it being taken away as quickly as it came. After Jayden journals a bit about this, she makes the connection that this shift in their relationship is bringing up her prioritization wound. After Jayden does the work to validate this wound and review whether it's the right time to speak up, she decides to communicate her feelings to Lani. But how?

Reread this story and on a separate sheet of paper, write down the feelings, thoughts, and actions Jayden is experiencing. See if you can identify a self-limiting belief and an invalidating message, and make a hypothesis about a core fear.

With some practice and choosing a good time to talk, Jayden ends up saying to her partner the next time they're face-to-face: "I thought I was prepared for this shift, but, when school finally started, I had a lot more anxiety than I realized. I started to miss you and then felt sad about losing some of the things we used to do. I even started to worry that you no longer cared for me the way you used to when we first started dating. I realized this wasn't all about you and me. It reminded me of my mom when I was growing up—how when she wasn't busy, she was a great mom. Then, when she'd get busy, it's like she forgot about me. I think somewhere deep inside, I'm worried that's going to happen with you."

Now, let's do the same thing for a personal experience of yours. See if you can link your current issue with a childhood wound of yours. Reflect on how that childhood wound has made you feel, think, and behave during this issue. This doesn't have to be a fully formed understanding or a perfect connection between past and present. This exercise is about *how* we talk about our wounds to our partners and loved ones in ways that are relevant today.

You can download these questions and respond to them at http://www.newharbinger.com/54384.

- What childhood wound is getting triggered?

- What did my partner or loved one do that triggered me?

- What did I think in response? What did I feel? What did I do?

- How does my childhood wound connect to this experience?

- What do I most want my partner/loved one to know about how this experience connects to my wound?

Practice saying your responses in the mirror. Don't worry—I'm not going to tell you to say this to anyone but yourself until you decide you are ready. However, it is super important to get comfortable talking vulnerably in this way if we want to be deeply understood. Many of us invalidate ourselves by thinking things like, *But isn't that too intense?* or *I don't want to make my problem theirs!* Remind yourself: Communicating about who you are and the wounds you carry is not making your problem theirs. It is taking ownership of your wounds and finding an effective way to shed light on them for those you love. Although this can be scary, more often than not, I've found that this way of communicating with loved ones can be met with understanding and empathy for what you experienced as a child and how that impacts you as an adult. When our loved ones know where our pain comes from, they can have the insight to show up differently. And, if your partner struggles to provide you with compassion, curiosity, and understanding, that is also important information for you to have.

Identifying Needs Related to Your Childhood Wounds

We've done a lot of work identifying needs. First, we identified our more surface needs, then we categorized needs versus wants, and now we are identifying needs that are directly related to our childhood wounds and may arise on a day-to-day basis when we are interacting with loved ones.

It is important to consider that while a satisfying relationship can be *supportive* of our wounds, it is unrealistic to expect that our adult relationships will completely *heal* our childhood wounds. This is where we must build our own capacity to tend to our own wounds alongside asking for what we need from others.

At http://www.newharbinger.com/54384, you'll find an exercise that asks you to choose childhood wounds that resonate most with you. You'll identify what fears stem from this wound, what you need from your loved one, and when you need this most. Next, you'll craft a mantra you can use to help tend to your wound. Finally, you'll brainstorm other things that can give you what you need to feel worthy, belonging, prioritized, and so on.

Just because we ask for a need does not mean our partner is always willing or able to meet it. Later in the book, we will discuss how to compromise when our needs conflict with our loved ones, needs. Considering our partner and loved ones' needs requires us to be deep listeners.

Listening Deeply

So much of what we have worked on has been about building your relationship to yourself. Now we are going to use all the work we've done to attend to another person. One of the biggest issues in our world today is how easy it is to get distracted. With our overdependence on smartphones, loved ones are complaining more than ever about a lack of connection when they are together.

Even though we've done all this work to heal wounds, if we struggle to be fully present with our loved ones, or if they struggle to be present with us, it won't matter how much work we've done. Imagine it's the first time you are trying to communicate with your partner about how your childhood wounds show up in your relationship, and, midway through, they respond to a text. It would feel pretty terrible, right? It would probably make you less likely to let yourself be vulnerable in the future.

Most of us know what it feels like to be deeply listened to, but we don't always know the ingredients of how or why we feel like that. In fact, active listening is one of the main aspects of communication that people who come into my practice struggle with. A lack of listening is the key thing that stops us from deeply understanding, practicing empathy, and building deep connections—all of which we need to do if we want to build and maintain healthy relationships.

EXERCISE: Active Listening

Together with your loved one, devote twenty minutes to this exercise (Robertson 2005; Gottman, Gottman, and DeClaire 2006). Minimize distractions—turn off the TV, put away your phones. One person will be the speaker, the other person will be the listener, and then you'll switch roles.

The first speaker will tell a brief story about their childhood; a minute or so is fine. It doesn't have to be a sad story, it can be happy or neutral. The listener's job is to deeply listen, which includes:

- facing and making eye contact with the speaker;

- using nonverbal communication, like nodding, to indicate their attention;

- mirroring the speaker's reactions (when the speaker smiles, smile back; when the speaker communicates a tough time, match their facial expression or body language);

- conveying interest (we all know what it feels like when you are boring someone with what you're saying; show your partner you care about what they're saying);

- listening for *total* meaning (often we listen only for content but to *deeply* listen means listening for the *feelings* experienced by the speaker about the content; ask yourself: *What* meaning *are they making from this experience?*).

Once the story is over, it is the listener's turn to speak.

First, thank them for sharing. Then, summarize the *content* of what you heard. Following that, summarize the *emotions* the speaker shared. Start with, "What it sounds like you felt was..." Then check if you are accurate. Ask, "Did I get that right?" Then ask more questions. Here is where you want to get really curious, almost like you are a cross between a scientist and a journalist, tasked with learning all you can about the subject. First, ask clarifying questions for anything you didn't understand. Then, ask questions from a place of wanting to know more and seeking to better understand; for example:

- What happened after that?

- Have you often felt like that?

- What was that like for you?

- What do you wish had happened?

- What understanding did you walk away with?

Convey empathy and share your experience of listening. Say something like, "That sounds like it was really fun/hard/sad." Share what it was like for you to take in the speaker's story. Then, switch roles and do the exercise again.

Remember this exercise the next time your loved one wants to share something with you that they are struggling with. More often than not, we tend to immediately jump into problem solving. This is a really sweet instinct in a way—we want to take away their pain and suffering as soon as possible. The only problem is, we miss a real opportunity to give them what they may actually need, which is empathy and understanding.

Here are some phrases to convey empathy if you get stuck, or if your loved one gets stuck and you need to give them an example of the empathy *you* need to hear:

- I'm here for whatever you need.

- That sounds so frustrating.

- I'm so sorry to hear that.

- I can't imagine what that must have been like. How are you doing with it?

- Tell me more.

- That makes complete sense.

- Thank you so much for sharing that.

- I can feel what you're saying in my own body.

- I don't even know what to say, but I'm so glad you told me.

Where did you struggle with this? Where did you excel? Reflect on this exercise so you each know where your strengths are and where you need to do some work.

Listening is a wonderful way to build closeness, and we simply don't always have the capacity to show up for our partners and loved ones in this way. Building a trusting relationship requires us to know when we can really dig into our partner's experience and when we cannot. This is where boundaries come in.

Setting Healthy Boundaries

It is just as important to determine what we *do* need as it is to determine what we don't need in our partnerships. Boundaries are clear guidelines that are established to help you clearly communicate the behavior you will and will not accept from your loved ones. Founder of the Embodiment Institute, Prentis Hemphill (2024) has my all-time favorite saying regarding boundaries: "Boundaries are the distance at which I can love you and me simultaneously."

Boundaries get a bad rap—we often worry we are being mean, selfish, and cold when we put them in place. However, putting boundaries in place helps us give to others from a place of genuine desire as opposed to from fear of potential repercussions. Giving from fear isn't really giving at all. When we show up for our loved ones from a place of desire, it is a wonderful gift that they can be sure we are giving because we *want* to and have the capacity to do. Boundaries build trust.

When we are in a relationship, we have boundaries for ourselves and for the relationship, and our partner has their own set of boundaries. Everyone has their own comfort level when it comes to boundaries.

Boundaries can be restrictions, like agreeing not to go through one another's phones, or psychological, like not commenting on what each other eats. We can create boundaries around the amount of time spent together, the frequency of communication, what is considered cheating, and what comments are below the belt in an argument. In relationships, boundaries can be a guideline rather than a decree, especially when partners have conflicting boundaries. In chapter 6, you'll find support around navigating these conflicts.

When we have childhood wounds, especially ones that cause us to suppress our true desires, we can overaccommodate, overfunction, avoid conflict, do things for others to prove our worth, or prevent ourselves from feeling guilty. These actions often lead to resentment because they are counter to what we actually want to do. Author and self-care expert Cheryl Richardson has often been quoted as saying, "If you avoid conflict to keep the peace, you start a war inside yourself." This is where boundary setting and later on, assertive communication come into play.

Let's look at the different types of boundaries you have in your current relationship or the types of boundaries you had (or wish you had) in your last relationship. These boundaries may be overarching or day-to-day. At http://www.newharbinger.com/54384, you can download a form with lines for adding your own ideas.

Physical boundaries: What are you not willing to engage in related to your physical body and physical environment?

Example: not wanting physical touch on a first date, wanting to live together (or not), wanting your partner to ask for consent before making a physical advance

Sexual boundaries: What are you not willing to engage in related to your sexual practices?

Example: not wanting to engage in a sexual practice without using protection, not wanting to engage in sexual activity one particular evening

Emotional boundaries: What are you not willing to engage in related to your emotional needs?

Example: not wanting your partner to raise their voice in anger, not wanting to share certain personal information, not wanting your partner to vent about their work stressors every day

Material boundaries: What are you not willing to engage in related to your material possessions (including finances)?

Example: not wanting to share a bank account until you're living together, saying no to going out for a fancy dinner because you are trying to save for vacation

Time boundaries: What are you not willing to engage in as it relates to your time?

Example: needing space for a half hour after you get home, not wanting to respond to texts when you are out with your friends, having a standing commitment to exercise on Wednesday evenings

Remember, boundaries aren't set in stone. You may have certain boundaries on your first few dates with someone, and those boundaries may shift as you get more comfortable. Or you may have certain boundaries for one person that you don't for another. You may have had to create some new boundaries following a breach of trust with your partner. A major life transition like the loss of a job or having a child may require you to revisit your own boundaries over time. Adapting to your shifting boundaries requires you to be able to validate that these shifts are legitimate, and being able to communicate these shifts to your loved ones is key.

It is important to note that only *you* can enforce your own boundary. For instance, if you don't want anyone to call you during working hours but your partner keeps calling, you are the only one who can fully enforce that boundary by not taking the call. However, it is very important to stay aware of those who continually make it difficult for us to respect our own boundaries. In these cases, you may have to distance yourself from these people.

Following childhood relational trauma, unhealthy boundaries that are too rigid or too penetrable often arise. In childhood, a rigid boundary might look like a parent using a domineering approach to their child or being a helicopter parent. Penetrable boundaries might be a parent treating their child like their best friend, using them as a sounding board to talk through their personal issues.

In adult relationships, rigid boundaries might look like immediately shutting down and refusing to discuss something when your partner has an issue. Sometimes our childhood wounds make us too inflexible; we have too many boundaries because we weren't priori-tized or we experienced a lot of deception or injustice. In these cases, it is important to consider whether this is a boundary you still need for your *current* relationship or whether you are trying to satisfy a wound that was created in your past. Allowing yourself to be influ-enced by your partner may be helpful. Penetrable boundaries might look like not being able to keep something a secret that your partner told you in confidence, or allowing all types of people the same level of access to your time and efforts despite a lack of reciprocity.

If you have experienced abuse and manipulation in your past, you may be susceptible to people using the term "boundary" to gain power and control over you. This could include restricting how you spend your time and money, and controlling whom you speak to and how you dress. Boundaries and control are not the same thing. When a loved one tries to use control to restrict or command your actions, this is unhealthy and can be a dangerous sign.

Communication Styles

In order to enforce boundaries, we need to practice assertive com-munication that decreases stress and improves our self-esteem (Pipas and Jaradat 2010). Depending on your childhood wounds, you may struggle with being too aggressive (especially when your fight response kicks in) or too passive (when your freeze or fawn response kicks in). Aggressive responses can bring about conflict and misun-derstanding; passive responses often deprioritize our needs and boundaries, which can lead us to making passive-aggressive com-ments or cause us to blow up at a later date.

Aggressive communication expresses one's needs and feelings while ignoring others' rights and boundaries. It can include accusa-tions, intimidation, criticism, or hostility (Bennett 2021). Passive communication avoids expressing one's needs, feelings, and values. Passive-aggressive communication is a blend of the two, a way to indirectly express negative feelings (Hall-Flavin 2024). Assertive communication, being polite yet firm and direct, is a happy medium. It considers your feelings; keeps in mind your boundaries, desires, and needs; and tries to find a middle ground between communication that is too forceful and communication that is too accommodating (Hill 2020). It asserts your needs and perspective while acknowledging others'.

Let's look at this scenario to consider the differences between these types of communication:

Your partner wants you to pick him up from the airport at 11 p.m. on Sunday so you can spend some time together before you start your work weeks. You have to wake up for work at 6 a.m. on Monday. You want to say no.

An aggressive response might sound like: "How can you expect me to pick you up when you know I have to wake up early the next day?"

A passive response might sound like: "Absolutely, can do!" (Meanwhile, you just texted your best friend about the situation, complaining that this is going to be a huge imposition for you.)

A passive-aggressive response might sound like: "I guess I could do that, though I do have to wake up early but I guess I'll figure it out."

An assertive response might sound like: "It doesn't look like I'm going to be able to do that because I have an early day tomorrow. I'd love to schedule some time to reconnect on Monday evening though, if you're able to!"

The first response is immediately going to put the other person on the defensive and has the greatest chance of starting an argument or leaving the other person to shut down and feel attacked or misunderstood. The passive response suggests that you don't *really* want to pick them up from the airport but you are ignoring your own needs in service of the other person. When someone deprioritizes their own needs and capacity over and over again, it can lead to frustration, resentment, and burnout. The assertive response considers your actual desires and also tries to find a happy medium that will satisfy both parties.

At http://www.newharbinger.com/54384, you find these two additional scenarios, with space for you to write in responses.

Scenario: *Your partner wants to reschedule your date for the second time in a row. You're disappointed because you were looking forward to it and frustrated because she canceled at the last minute.*

Scenario: *When having dinner together, your partner doesn't ask about your day, even though they knew you were set to give a big presentation. You just spent ten minutes talking about their day and now they are ready to turn on the television.*

Assertiveness is a wonderful way to respect your own needs, boundaries, and desires. It helps you show up authentically in your relationships and give from a place of true desire, instead of guilt or fear. It builds trust because your people know that you mean what you say and say what you mean: when you can't do something it is because you truly can't or don't want to, and when you can, it's because you genuinely want to. When we respond aggressively, it's often because we've crossed our own boundaries and need to remember that only we can enforce our own boundaries. Many people are passive until their capacity gets completely depleted and they skip straight to aggressive or become passive-aggressive. Assertiveness helps us stay steady and balanced by standing up for ourselves when we need to and showing people how to love and care for us.

Unfortunately, learning to practice assertiveness isn't always pretty. Enforcing boundaries and asserting your needs and desires may result in your loved ones feeling disappointed, frustrated, hurt, and even angry. One of the best things you can do to tend to your childhood wounds is to prepare yourself for these responses. Disappointing or hurting your partner may be incredibly triggering for you and may activate a wound. You may worry that they'll leave you, or that you're selfish for prioritizing a need. This is a moment to show yourself compassion and remind yourself that healing your wounds and breaking relational patterns is hard work. No one can get their needs met all the time, and sometimes your needs will be in direct conflict with a loved one's needs. In these cases, disappointment *will* happen but that doesn't mean you've done anything wrong. You are in the messy, uncomfortable middle of this journey. Repeat to yourself: *I am allowed to have needs and it is important that my loved one is aware of them. This is hard.*

When to Walk Away: The Six Questions

Boundaries not only help us get what we need from our loved ones but also determine the frequency with which we will engage with our loved ones if (or when) they repeatedly struggle to respect our boundaries. The less respect they have for our boundaries, the less frequently or intensely we may decide to engage with them. Perhaps you tell a friend something in confidence, and they tell other people. If they repeatedly demonstrate difficulty respecting your desire for privacy, a new boundary might be that you tell them less personal information going forward, even though you still maintain a friendship.

There are cases where, no matter what you do, you find yourself in a relationship that chronically leaves you feeling emotionally unsafe, dissatisfied, and unseen. This does not mean that something is wrong with you or that you deserve to feel this way. Unfortunately, trauma often begets more trauma. We talked early on about repetition compulsions: our tendency to repeat unhealthy patterns in the hope they will result in a different outcome where we feel more empowered and in control. Sadly, this means that sometimes we will find ourselves in relationships that do not satisfy our needs, just as we did not get certain needs met by our parents and caregivers. In these cases, we find ourselves on the merry-go-round of trying to get the same need met by someone who will never be able to meet it. In a social media interview, therapist Patrick Teahan says, "The mark of childhood trauma is trying to get a difficult person to be good to us." If you feel as called out by that statement as I do, you are not alone. But how do you know, *for sure*, that you are in one of those types of relationships?

Remember, you cannot *change* your loved one's behavior. You can only have an *impact* on it—through effective communication and working on how you respond to the behavior. Unfortunately, you may communicate a need that is central to your satisfaction in your relationship, and it might be ignored or your loved one may not have the desire or capacity to fulfill it. In this case, you may need to ask yourself some difficult questions.

Although many relationship struggles can be overcome, it is also important to know when it might be time to walk away. A framework that I often use for this is what I call the Six Questions. If you find yourself questioning whether it's time to walk away, think about an important need that is getting unmet in one of your close relationships. Be specific and write it down. Then, ask yourself:

1. Have I communicated the importance of this need?

2. Did I feel heard by my loved one?

3. Are they taking the steps to meet my needs?

4. Is there evidence of positive change? If so, what is the evidence?

5. What is *my part* of the issue; that is, what is something I have total control over in this situation? Am I taking steps to work on my part of the issue?

6. Are all of our efforts enough?

If you answer no to any of these questions, you have your starting point. For example, if you haven't communicated that this is an important need, doing that is your first task. If you haven't determined what *you* can do to help get this need satisfied, do some self-reflection on that.

That last question might feel really abstract. It's supposed to be. Only *you* can decide what "enough" looks and feels like for you. One person may decide that they can tolerate the time it might take for their partner to give them what they need; another person may decide they can't or won't wait that long based on a variety of factors. There is no right decision. There is only the right decision for you.

This might be upsetting or confrontational for you. It may bring up feelings of fear, guilt, exclusion, and abandonment. It is important to acknowledge the wounds getting dredged up as you go through this process, as the core fears tied to them may keep us in relationships for longer than is healthy for fear of rejection, isolation, guilt, unworthiness, and so on.

If you find yourself getting into the same relationship over and over again, one that doesn't give you what you need, I recommend adopting this mantra: *Just because I can doesn't mean I should.* You may have become very good at dealing with your partner's anger, or their tendency to shut down during hard conversations, or the chaos you feel due to their mental health or substance-use struggles. You may have gotten very good at dealing with this tendency because it is very similar to what you dealt with growing up. Part of healing is recognizing that just because you *can* navigate those waters (and have become very adept at that navigation) doesn't mean you *should* have to navigate them.

In order for a relationship to function, we have to be responsible for our own stuff. Only once we are responsible for our own stuff can we separate what is ours from what is theirs and be able to build a strong and stable foundation together.

Coregulation

In order to successfully commingle our stuff with our loved one's stuff in a way that doesn't cause an explosive chemical reaction, we can use one of the most beautiful relationship tools we have at our disposal: *coregulation*. Coregulation, or calming down together, is the ability for two people to both self-soothe in order to have a healthy and effective interaction despite there being big feelings at play. The powers of coregulation are scientifically proven—we feel calmer in the face of danger when we are comforted by a safe loved one (Coan, Schaefer, and Davidson 2006).

In previous chapters, we talked a lot about identifying and responding to triggers. However, we won't succeed at effectively responding to our triggers 100 percent of the time, nor will our loved ones. In fact, fights that feel terrible often happen because one person gets triggered, which activates their partner, which in turn exacerbates the triggers, and the vicious cycle continues until both people feel out of control.

With coregulation, we can spot our own activation as well as our partner's, and we can mindfully, in the present moment, help each other calm down before we say and do hurtful things. So many of us have wounds *because* our parents and caregivers weren't able to use this tool during our childhood. As a result, we may not have learned how to regulate ourselves.

Try the following coregulation activities with a partner or loved one. Practice these exercises when you are not in conflict so that when you do get into conflict you will have already had some experience with them.

- *Cobreathing:* Sit facing each other on the ground with your legs crossed. Take deep breaths in through your nose and let them out through your mouth. Breathe in for four seconds and out for eight seconds, stimulating your vagus nerve, the nerve that helps calm you down.

- *Ball toss:* When you are having a logistical conversation that requires problem solving, toss a ball underhand back and forth. The back-and-forth motion promotes coordination and movement, which will keep the two of you emotionally and physiologically regulated.

Practice the next two exercises when one or both of you are stressed or overwhelmed, or you are having a difficult conversation:

- *Heart touch:* Hug your partner with your chests touching, or each take the palm of your hand and put them over one another's heart. Each breathe deeply. Don't stop until you feel your breathing sync up.

- *Changing your environment:* During your tough conversation, notice when one or both of you are in need of a break. (Refer back to chapter 3, where you learned about your body state when it feels triggered. Is your face getting hot? Do you feel like you want to cry?) Call a time-out from the conversation, and change your environment; for example, blast some cheerful music and have a dance party, do jumping jacks, or splash your faces with cold water. Revisit the conversation only when you both feel calmer. Change things up as often as you need to throughout the conversation.

If you already have self-soothing techniques that you use when you need to calm down, that's wonderful. Does your partner know what those are? Do you know what your partner's self-soothing strategies are? Don't discount how powerful it can be to get a warm and helpful reminder from your partner to take a deep breath when they notice that you're getting activated. Even just their hand on your shoulder or back can be a helpful cue to take a minute to calm down. These cues help you both be accountable to one another's regulation, which signals that you want to show up as your very best for one another.

Repairing After Fights

We've done a lot of work in this chapter to both prevent fights from occurring and learn how to engage in conflict in healthier ways. Unfortunately, the reality is that fights will still happen even when we're trying our very best. Try not to see getting into fights as a failure. In fact, it's often a red flag when a couple reports that they don't *ever* experience conflict because that can suggest that there's a lack of safety in bringing up hard thoughts and feelings. Consider that fights will occur and that one of the most important aspects to a healthy relationship isn't how often you fight, it's how you fight and if you repair following the fight (Gottman, Gottman, and DeClaire 2006).

It can be very tempting to pretend our fights didn't happen once they're done. Especially if we acted in less than mature ways, it might be very appealing to chalk the fight up to a bad moment and keep moving on. However, when we move on too quickly from fights without learning from them and taking accountability for our words and actions, hurts can pile up. An awful thing you might have said to your partner in anger is now sitting with them, and even if you are positive they know you don't feel like that, over time, negativity and criticism during conflict will erode their trust and sense of safety with you. You may find that you or your partner have stopped bringing issues up over time. When fights don't go well and we never seem to walk away with learnings or a clear plan of what to do differently, we stop leaning into conflict because it simply doesn't feel useful. Eventually, disconnection and isolation set in. We begin to keep the peace at all costs instead of speaking up and solving problems proactively.

Taking accountability for what we did wrong during a fight is instrumental in creating safe and healthy partnerships. This can be incredibly hard to do if it was never modeled to you as a child. In fact, experiencing a chronic lack of accountability from loved ones is a theme I've seen in adults who experienced childhood relational trauma. For many of us, it isn't just the traumatic experiences that were harmful, it was our parents' and family members' inability to *name* the wrongdoing, apologize, commit to doing better, and show evidence of doing better. Instead, many have received opposite responses when they've discussed their childhood wounds with their parents and caregivers, such as, "You act like your childhood was terrible!" or "I don't remember ever doing that!" or "I guess I was a horrible parent then!"

When these are the responses you get from someone who has hurt you, a cycle repeats. First, good old invalidation has occurred. We now know this invalidation gets internalized, and we have learned how to identify it within ourselves. It sounds like, "Maybe I *am* making too big a deal out of things." Thus, *we* never learn how to take a healthy amount of accountability for our wrongdoing when someone brings their hurts to *our* attention, setting us up for generational trauma. In fact, many folks with childhood wounds see their mistakes as evidence that their self-limiting beliefs are true—that they are in fact bad people or unlovable, so the idea of taking accountability is something too painful to bear. Remember, we repeat what we see. If we don't grow up learning how to take accountability, we may respond defensively and as though we played no role in the wrongdoing. Or we may have learned to take too much accountability. In those cases, we may take too much responsibility and continue to overfunction, forgetting that there is another person who needs to acknowledge their piece of the puzzle.

Taking accountability is brave, but it also pays dividends in our relationships. Our partners and loved ones learn, through our actions, that we are safe because we are accountable for our wrongdoing and are committed to working on our flaws. When our partners cannot depend on this, or when we cannot depend on this in our partners, overcoming problems together is very difficult.

The Steps of Accountability

The next time you are in a conflict, go through these accountability steps:

1. Talk about what happened from your perspective. Taking turns, practice your active-listening skills and impact statements from chapter 3.

2. Communicate that you see one another's perspective as valid even if you don't agree. Don't get into trying to recount the truth of what happened; doing that can reignite the fight. You each have versions of the truth and will remember different parts in different ways. You do not have to sign on to your loved one's realities in order to empathize or be curious about them. If you don't understand, ask questions to better understand, not as a way to prove your point.

3. Take specific accountability for the role you played in this conflict. What did *you* do that made it worse? Be careful to not follow this up with blame—"I wouldn't have acted that way if you weren't so difficult!" The statement of accountability should stand alone. This can be very difficult, especially if you haven't practiced.

Breathe through making your statement, and remind yourself that we all make mistakes. Mean what you say. Make eye contact when you're speaking.

4. Reflect on and communicate what you'd like to do differently going forward. Maybe you waited too long to bring something up and then you exploded. That might mean you'll consider bringing your issue up earlier. Elicit feedback from your partner; see if they have any suggestions.

5. Be kind when your partner is being accountable. Again, if you grew up in a house with manipulation or emotional abuse, you may have learned that the person who takes accountability loses. *Yay! I won the argument,* you think. *Now I'll double down and really make them pay.* Resist the urge to do this. Remember that taking accountability makes us vulnerable, and we want to give our partner a soft landing so they will feel safe to do this again in the future. Treat them the way you want to be treated when taking accountability.

Putting It All Together

You just did some seriously hard and scary work. I cannot tell you how many times someone tells me that they have to heal on their own before they get into relationships. I completely understand the urge to cocoon ourselves away until we emerge into a fully healed butterfly, ready to choose the right partners and say all the right things.

However, the reality is that because our deepest wounds come from our relationships, our most transformative healing will come from being in relation with others. I can't think of anything more terrifying than knowing our healing requires us to open ourselves up to the world around us and connect authentically, keeping self-love at the forefront. Please remember that your relationships are a mirror showing you what areas you still need to heal. From doing the work in the last chapter, you have a toolbox to carry with you into your relationships that takes into account your healing. In this chapter, you gained the tools for how to do that while in relation to another. You now know when to speak up, how to share your wounding, how to listen deeply, how to set boundaries, how to assertively communicate, when to walk away, how to coregulate, and how to repair with accountability. Well done, you! Next, you are going to go deeper into communication strategies to learn how to solve problems.

CHAPTER 6

Problem Solve

While learning how to communicate effectively is imperative to your own well-being and the well-being of your relationships, talking about your needs, fear, issues, and desires is only half the battle. For you to feel deeply satisfied within your relationships, you and your loved one need to feel confident and competent at solving problems together.

Many of us have the same fights repeatedly with our loved ones. The content may be different each time but the underlying fears, desires, and frustrations remain relatively constant. When you learn how to creatively and collaboratively solve problems with your loved ones, you are acting as a team to forge a new path forward.

Do You Have What You Need?

In order to solve problems with our loved ones, we have to know what we need or what is most important to us. We can start to think about our needs hierarchically. When we do this, we can clue our partner in to what is imperative for us as opposed to what is simply nice to have. In order to have this conversation, we need to build self-awareness around our hierarchy of needs first.

To start, we have basic survival needs that must be met before we can seek and receive higher-level needs, which consider emotions, identity, and purpose. Psychologist Abraham Maslow (1943) organized our individual needs with physiological needs at the foundation and self-actualization at the top:

- Physiological needs: clothing, air, water, food, clothing, shelter, sleep

- Safety needs: security and freedom from danger

- Love and belonging needs: intimate friendships and relationships

- Esteem needs: prestige and a feeling of accomplishment

- Self-actualization needs: achieving one's full potential

If our physiological needs aren't met, it becomes more difficult and unrealistic to get our love and belonging needs met and ultimately our need to self-actualize. Considering this framework when you are solving problems can help you be more intentional in communicating what you need and when.

When we get into fights with our partner, it's helpful to pause and consider if your physiological needs have been met. If you are struggling with food and housing insecurity, working on your relationship will likely feel out of reach until your basic needs become stabilized. Perhaps your basic needs are generally met, but not at this exact moment. When was the last time you ate or drank water? Did you ever find yourself thinking that everything is horrible and then have a snack or take a walk and realize things aren't so bad after all?

Perhaps it's your safety needs that need attention. Perhaps you are in a relationship that makes you feel physically or emotionally unsafe. Because many of us grew up in physically or emotionally unsafe situations, these dynamics might feel familiar but that doesn't mean that they are okay. You may not even have considered that, at a basic level, you deserve to feel safe, respected, valued, and secure. If you are experiencing a pattern of feeling belittled, controlled, intimidated, frightened, or isolated by your partner, you may be in an abusive relationship. Consider that there are even culturally normalized behaviors, such as guilt tripping, that can fall under the umbrella of emotional abuse. If your partner or loved one is exhibiting behaviors that make you feel like you need to act in certain ways to be loved, this is a problematic dynamic. Focusing on this issue is often the first place to start.

If this resonates with you, seeking out professional support, building your self-worth, and leaning on your community is imperative. If you are experiencing abuse in your relationship, you are not alone and it is not your fault. For support and to learn more, visit the website of the National Domestic Violence Hotline (http://www .thehotline.org) or call 1-800-799-SAFE.

You might be upset with your partner for not being supportive, but when you do some self-reflection you realize you're actually upset because you miss the community of friends you had during college. Instead of expecting your partner to be your everything, you may decide that you need to seek out more friendships. You may be in conflict with your partner because they didn't come to an event that was important for you. After reflecting on Maslow's hierarchy, you realize that this event is tied to your self-esteem. Suddenly, the conflict stops being about how your partner prioritizes work over you, and you start to share that their lack of attendance was most disappointing because the event was a source of great self-esteem for you. Using Maslow's hierarchy reminds us that we need to check in with ourselves and what our needs *represent* before we can problem solve solutions with another.

The Sound Relationship House

Therapist John Gottman built upon Maslow's theory with his Sound Relationship House for a secure partnership. He imagined that relationships were like a house that both people build in order to create a strong structure. Trust and commitment are the walls of the house, the two central pillars that create the outer structure of the home. Each floor has a focus that needs to be tended to in order to have a strong, freestanding home. If there are deficits in any given floor, that is where the couple needs to focus on in order to rebuild (Gottman and Silver 1999; Gottman, Gottman, and DeClaire 2006).

As you review these floors, keep an important relationship in mind. Which floors do you feel like you need to repair?

Floor 1: Build love maps

> Learn about one another. Do you know one another's likes and dislikes? Hopes and dreams? Favorite movies? What brings your partner the most stress at work? What are their pet peeves?

Floor 2: Share fondness and admiration

> Verbalize the characteristics that you appreciate in your partner. Gottman believes in striving for a ratio of one complaint or negative interaction to five compliments or positive interactions. If you grew up in a very critical household or have a worthiness wound, receiving and giving positive affirmations can be deeply healing and satisfying, although difficult to master.

Floor 3: Turn toward

> When you or your partner make a bid for connection or response to a need, you have three options: turn toward, turn away, or reject the bid. Ideally, we want to be turning toward our partner's need for connection as often as possible. Turning away from our partner's bids can have drastic consequences, especially when we carry abandonment or prioritization wounds.

Floor 4: Positive perspective

This means seeing the best in each other and giving one another the benefit of the doubt. This can be especially difficult if you have a trust wound, as you may find yourself hypervigilant, always waiting for the other shoe to drop to protect yourself.

Floor 5: Manage conflict

Knowing what to do during conflict is key. Accepting your partner's influence and viewing conflict as collaborative is key. You may never have seen healthy conflict growing up, especially if there was constant fighting or you lived in a house where problems were swept under the rug.

Floor 6: Make life dreams come true

Supporting each another to reach your hopes, dreams, and goals creates a partnership where you help the other person be who they want to be. This might look like supporting their desire to go back to school or run a half-marathon. This is also a place where many conflicts occur because they touch on our deeper hopes and dreams. The more intimately we know what those are for our partners, the easier it will be to spot when these get threatened during a conflict.

Floor 7: Create shared meaning

These are the rituals, inside jokes, and symbols you create together that build an inner world in your partnership. This shared culture makes your relationship unique and meaningful.

When we are in conflict, especially when there are emotions involved, solving problems can often feel like throwing spaghetti at a wall to see what sticks. By keeping in mind Maslow's and Gottman's frameworks, you can consider when you need to attend to a core need. For instance, if you feel ignored or disrespected by your partner, it may be unrealistic for you to be working on building more sexual intimacy; instead you need to focus on building trust and commitment. If you feel like strangers who have changed drastically since the beginning of your relationship, you may need to start by getting to know each other again.

When you think about your relationship, or a past relationship that brought you turmoil, think about which floor you need to tend to now, or which floor you wish had been tended to back then. If you have identified a floor that needs more attention in a current relationship, make a plan with your partner to spend some time on that floor this week.

The Problem-Solving Process

Solving problems becomes more difficult when our relationship is deep. Over time, our patterns of thinking, feeling, and behaving become like well-worn grooves in a machine. We start to make assumptions about our loved ones—we think, *Oh, he would never go for that!* or *She would totally freak out if I brought that up.* When we make these assumptions, they create limiting beliefs that set us along a path of taking the same steps of the pattern we've always followed. Psychologist Sue Johnson (2004) calls this pattern a "dance." You do this, they do that, you respond, they respond. Seemingly simple problems become gridlocked and insurmountable, not because they are too complicated to solve, but because our way of seeing the issue makes them *feel* unsolvable.

When we use a simple problem-solving process, we go back to the basics. This process may seem rudimentary, but I promise you, it can get very complicated very quickly when our wounds, self-limiting beliefs, and fears get invited to the party.

EXERCISE: Step-by-Step Problem Solving

Think of a problem you are having with a partner or loved one.

Step 1: Identify the problem.

This can be the hardest step. Often, we identify only a piece of the problem, or we make an interpretation around the problem like, *He just doesn't seem to care about me!* Instead, identify a problem that you both agree is the problem. Make it as factual as possible. If you are having trouble, sometimes the problem might even be: *She thinks this is a problem, but I don't see what the issue is. That's* the problem in that scenario.

Step 2: Brainstorm solutions.

This is a collaborative process. Make sure not to discount any suggestions as stupid or not likely to work. This step is a time for pure exploration. Write down the solutions if that would be helpful. Get creative. Imagine what's possible together.

Step 3: Choose a solution.

As a team, pick one of the solutions to try.

Step 4: Give that solution a try.

See how it goes. Be careful not to view this effort through a black-and-white lens by telling yourself that either it worked or it didn't. Notice what worked and what didn't work about that solution.

Step 5: Discuss and debrief.

Come back together and discuss how it went. What did you both like? Not like? Do you need to go back to the drawing board? If so, revisit your previous list of solutions. Try something else and go through step 4 again until the problem is solved. Or perhaps you have identified a new problem that needs solving. In that case, start at the beginning and go through the steps again.

To make this step-by-step guide easily accessible for repeated use, you can download it at http://www.newharbinger.com/54384.

Reaching a Compromise

Our relationship problems sometimes require us to strike compromises. This can be difficult because we may struggle with being too rigid or too flexible. It can be very hard to discern when you are making necessary and healthy adjustments for the good of your relationship and when you are compromising on your fundamental needs and identity. Conversely, it can be hard to determine when you are holding onto a boundary that is no longer serving you, but your upbringing has made you feel like things need to be this way because they always have been.

One area I see couples struggle with is viewing their problem as win or lose, with a focus on getting the other person to come to their side. When we approach problems like this, compromise is impossible because we are already starting the conversation from a place of there being only one version of "right." In compromise, it is imperative to validate the experience and reality of *both* people. Only then can we see both sides as legitimate and work toward meeting somewhere in the middle. When you think, *Well, they're just being ridiculous,* or *Well, they just need to change,* compromise is not possible.

Instead, dig deeper, tapping into both your needs, fears, and feelings, and your partner's. This is similar to linking our needs to our core wounds. Revisit chapters 3 and 4 first if needed.

Then, grab your partner or loved one and choose an issue that you want to compromise on. Write it down on a separate sheet of paper where you both can see it. Like we did with active listening and seeking to understand, take turns being the speaker and listener for the questions below (adapted from Gottman 2006). Ask follow-up questions if you don't understand your loved one's answer. Switch roles when you have completed these questions for one person.

Ask each other these questions, using your active listening skills:

- What makes this situation so important to you?

- What is your ideal scenario?

- What is an experience from your past that is related to this situation?

- What are you most afraid of related to this situation not going the way you want?

- Does this relate to a belief, value, purpose, or goal you have?

After you are finished, reflect on what you learned about your loved one's view of the situation that you didn't already know.

Next, identify the area you need to compromise on. See if you need to change or relabel it at all based on the conversation you both had.

Now, let's focus on the space between your side and your partner's view of what needs compromising. This is where we can get into win/lose framing when, in reality, there is a much larger space between the two sides than we realized. Let's say Sal wants to go to a party and Jack doesn't. There are many more options than simply staying home or going to the party, even though it may initially feel like there aren't. Jack and Sal can go to the party for a shorter amount of time. Sal can go and Jack can stay home. Both can go and Jack can leave early. Both can decide not to go and then do something social the next day. Both can decide not to go but invite the hosts over for dinner next weekend. See? So many more options. The way we determine what other options there are is to really tap into what is most important to each person.

Revisit the issue you labeled that needs compromising. On a separate sheet of paper, each person writes a column of what areas they are flexible around and what areas they are not flexible around (Gottman 2006). Consider frequency, intensity, and duration. Use your brainstorming skills here.

In the party example, let's say that Sal is inflexible around showing up (meaning he absolutely has to) but is flexible around how long they stay. What is most important to Jack is getting up early the next day to study for an upcoming exam. Jack lets Sal know that he is inflexible about staying out past ten but is flexible about going to the party. They decide to go to the party but leave before ten. Tapping into what is most important helps us be creative and responsive in our problem solving.

If you are struggling to get to a solution, write down any core fears, self-limiting beliefs, or invalidating statements that might be getting in the way. Maybe Jack is thinking: *We always do what Sal wants to do! This time it's my turn!* Or he could be thinking: *Why am I making such a big deal of this? It's so silly.* These are the beliefs *about* the issue that make problem solving difficult. You may need to start by validating your feelings or describing what you're afraid of. In Jack's case, it may be saying: "I'm having a hard time budging here because I feel like I'm always the one to make concessions."

Next, share your areas of flexibility and inflexibility with one another. See if you can come up with a list of solutions based on these areas. If things get emotionally heated during this process, take a time-out: agree on for how long you will take space (at least five minutes, no more than twenty minutes) and when you will reconnect. While taking space, do something relaxing and try not to think about this process. If one person is ready to reconnect and the other isn't, agree on how much more time you will give each other. This is especially important for anxious/avoidant couples. It may be difficult for the anxious person to self-soothe, while it may be difficult for the avoidant person to want to revisit the conversation. We will go deeper into this during the next exercise. You can use this time-out process at any time during a conflict.

When you've reconnected, choose a compromise that you both feel motivated to try, bringing the same experimental energy you brought to the problem-solving process. Debrief afterward. What worked in this compromise this time? What didn't? If the compromise didn't feel like a satisfying solution, try another one the next time you do this exercise.

Avoiding Conflict

When we're in a conflict, it's tempting to avoid the problem to keep peace. This is highly problematic as it not only robs us from being our true selves but also stops us from getting our needs met in our most intimate relationships, leading to feelings of isolation and disconnection. Depending on our childhood wounds, avoiding conflict can become a painful self-fulfilling prophecy, making us feel fundamentally unworthy of getting the love we deserve.

The way to counter this is by digging into it with our loved ones, leaning into the conflict and ultimately creating stronger bonds. This is no easy feat—it takes bravery, fortitude, and a belief that things can be different, better.

To learn about your conflict-avoidance behaviors, do some journaling on a separate sheet of paper using the prompts that follow. You can also download them at http://www.newharbinger.com/54384.

What emotions do you experience when you are likely to avoid a situation?

What are you thinking when you are avoiding a situation? For example, *What's the point?* or *This isn't a big deal.*

What behaviors from others cause you to avoid a situation? For example, when you share a feeling and the other person reacts defensively, or when you refrain from certain behaviors that you've heard your partner criticize in others.

What are you looking for or do you need the most from yourself when you are avoiding a situation? From your loved ones?

I challenge you to be brave and share some of these reflections with your partner. Have a conversation about what you learned and give them an opportunity to better understand. This sharing will support you in moments of conflict when your urge is to avoid by fleeing or freezing from stress.

Relapse Prevention

You have learned so much about yourself in order to enhance your relationship to yourself and others. Well done! Next, we need to consider that progress is not a straight line. In reality, when we try to make necessary positive changes in our lives, our progress looks more like a rollercoaster, with peaks and valleys. Ultimately, we hope that there will be more peaks than valleys, but we also need to prepare for inevitable setbacks in our progress.

One of the more damaging parts of taking steps backward, or having relapses, is the way we view those relapses when they occur. It can be very tempting to think, *Well, now I'm back to square one!* or *See? I knew it wouldn't last!* but these are self-limiting beliefs. Human nature is complicated. We are not robots that set a goal and make progress each day until we reach it. We have to make space for new life stressors, dips in our mood and energy, and unforeseen barriers that arise. What we want to do is to prepare for inevitable relapses to occur, acknowledge our setbacks, feel the feelings that arise from these setbacks, and get back on track. But how?

First, let's identify the areas that you are trying to make progress in. Think about all the reflecting you have done in this book, and choose two specific areas that you want to work on. Maybe you are trying to invalidate yourself less or practice more positive self-talk. Maybe you are trying to respond less defensively when your partner has an issue. Maybe you are trying to communicate your needs more often while dating. Maybe you are trying to shut down less when you and your partner have fights. Write these development areas down on a separate sheet of paper under the heading Stuff I'm Working On, or use the template you can download at http://www.newhar binger.com/54384.

For each area, list all the ways in which you are likely to experience a relapse. Consider life stressors and your upcoming calendar, as well as more emotional and psychological considerations impacting your ability to stay on track. For example, if you're working on eating healthier, a relapse might be going out drinking, which often leads you to crave salty and fatty foods. If you're working on defensiveness, consider that not feeling connected to your partner might result in even more defensiveness later on. If you are trying to invalidate yourself less, consider that hanging out with other people who struggle to validate themselves might impact you.

Now develop your relapse plan by brainstorming and writing down ideas about what *you* can do to minimize the potential for relapses to occur. Be careful not to skip this plan. I often see over-confidence when it comes to shifting behaviors: *I just won't do it* or *It really shouldn't be this hard!* I often hear people sorely underestimating how much their present environment and their psychology lead them to repeatedly behave in ways they wish they wouldn't.

Proactively and intentionally planning out what we need before relapses occur is a wonderful way to guard against the shame, guilt, hopelessness, apathy, and demotivation that come along with relapses. For healthy eating, it's helpful to stock the pantry with healthier snack options so you can be set up for success. What things can you do to set yourself up for success to continue working on your stuff? Where will you need help from another? Maybe you and your partner agree on a code word that reminds you to take a deep breath, and use it when one of you notices the other's defensiveness.

The danger of relapses is that, when they inevitably occur, we can have an *Oh, to hell with it!* attitude. If you "slip up" by having some potato chips, it's common to think, *Well, I've ruined my streak so I might as well eat the whole bag!* Instead, list the thoughts, feelings, and behaviors that may arise when relapses occur. Ask yourself: *How will I treat myself and talk to myself kindly, in a way that maintains my motivation when relapses inevitably occur?*

After you have finished writing, communicate this relapse plan to your partner or loved one. Accountability partners can be instrumental in helping us reach our goals. We all need cheerleaders—both the cheerleaders we practice being for ourselves and the loved ones who build us back up when we fall down.

Self-Care

It is nearly impossible to sustain my emotionally taxing job if I am not taking care of myself. In fact, therapists often use the example of an oxygen mask on an airplane, reminding us that if you want to help people, you need to put your own oxygen mask on first. The same premise goes for relationships. If you do not take care of yourself, it is near impossible to be able to adequately care for your relationships. And yet, so many of us who hold identities known for nurturing have internalized messages that require us to deprioritize ourselves to maintain the status quo. When we consider what brings about a relapse—whether you're trying to yell less during fights or working on saying no more often—not having a clear and consistent plan for how to take care of yourself will make it very difficult to reach your goals of healing your wounds. Say you're trying to acknowledge your partner's efforts more. If you feel depleted and burned out, there is a very low chance that you will be able to see the opportunity, let alone verbalize the acknowledgment you are working on practicing. It is much more likely you're thinking, *When is someone going to notice how much I do around here?*

Imagine the flip side—two people in a partnership who already have their buckets filled by hobbies, purpose, and other satisfying connections. When we are fulfilled, it is far more likely that we'll give someone we love the benefit of the doubt or stay curious when they've made a mistake. Regularly practicing self-care is some of the best relapse prevention we have. In that simple sentence, I am giving you permission to get that monthly massage or take that trip. Your relationships may depend on it!

You are not alone if you draw a blank when I ask, "What's your self-care practice?" So many people have never considered that there are activities that make us feel happy, relaxed, nurtured, connected, energized, or simply like *ourselves.* Engaging in regular self-care is one way to create more protective factors so that when life inevitably brings hardship, these hardships don't feel as monumental or insurmountable.

Adopting a self-care practice first requires awareness around what you *already* do that feels good or true to yourself. Then, intentionally plan to do those things more often in specific circumstances (like getting a facial after a particularly stressful week) and build the awareness to listen when your body is telling you what you need (like noticing you're extra depleted and may need to reschedule social plans to recharge your battery).

Think about self-care as a *practice,* meaning that what you need will change. One week, self-care may look like scheduling time with your friends, the next week self-care looks like you spending the night alone to binge-watch a new show.

Using the chart you'll find at http://www.newharbinger.com/54384, write down what you already do, or could do, next to each of these seven pillars of self-care: mental, emotional, physical, environmental, spiritual, recreational, social. Next to each item, add how often you would ideally like to do those things. Maybe under *Mental* you like to do a crossword puzzle every morning and under *Spiritual* you like to volunteer once a month. Overlap is fine—volunteering might satisfy both your spiritual and social needs. Under *Social*, take special note of the people in your life who make you feel seen, who are gentle with your most vulnerable parts. As you engage socially, take note of the people who drain energy from you as well as those who make you feel energized.

It is very important to not make your self-care overly prescriptive, like a schedule. Self-care is not something we should feel guilty or shameful around because we haven't done "enough." Instead of doing self-care "perfectly," see it as a menu that you order from depending on what you are craving.

Conclusion: A Road Map for the Future

Congratulations! You've done the difficult work of learning how your past shapes your present, gaining a clearer picture of who you are and how you relate to others. Trauma is like living in the midst of a fog, obscuring your essentialness, along with your true wants, needs, and preferences. With the knowledge you've gained, you've not only cleared the fog but also gotten a more defined picture of the authentic you that exists beneath the haze versus who you had to become—the thoughts, feelings and behaviors you learned—to survive your childhood relational trauma. These learned parts of you helped you get through tough times in childhood but held you back from living the life and finding the loving relationships you deserve. Healing from trauma is both an unlearning and learning process—unlearning the parts of you that served as your protections from harm and learning how to access your truest self now that you've grown into an adult who can give the care you needed and deserved, back then and to this very day.

As you know now, trauma not only impacts how we see the world but also how we see ourselves. Unfortunately, there is no checklist for healing from trauma. Your life will not be split into two parts: before healing and after healing. Instead, your healing will continue as you find the individual and relational moments to break the patterns no longer serving you. In this way, some relationships have the potential to be a continuation of your trauma while others can help you heal. With the work you just did, you have the ability to seek relationships that confirm what *everyone* deserves to feel and know deep in their bones: we are all worthy of love and care as we are today, both from our loved ones and most importantly from ourselves.

Many people are looking for great partners as well as lifelong friendships. As we conclude our work together, remember that people don't show up in our lives as fully formed beings who are perfect for us. Instead, it is in the give-and-take that healing relationships are created. It's the daily moments when you're brave enough to say that your feelings were hurt or to ask for some space. It's in doing the daily work of amplifying your truest self that you allow yourself to be seen. This book did not include a prescription for how to find perfect people. Instead, in becoming your truest self, you set yourself up to find people who are truly compatible with you. Few people are so fundamentally bad or broken that we have to stay vigilant to protect ourselves from them. Instead, by leaning sturdily on self-trust and the belief that we have the power to give ourselves what we need, we can simply see people for who they are and decide for ourselves if they have the qualities and abilities to build strong relationships with us.

Remembering that our caregivers were once children who also didn't get what they needed reminds us that we are all children who went without. This book puts a spotlight on some of your caregivers' behaviors. It is difficult to not feel big feelings about what you didn't get (and may continue to not get) and how that resulted in the person you became.

Having compassion for the child in all of us helps us take over what we can control (how you treat yourself now) and leave behind what you couldn't control (how you were treated as a child) in the past. You may always grieve for what you didn't receive. There is nothing in these pages that can completely take away the pain of going without the type of love and care you needed. When those waves of grief come, let them. You are entitled to feel that deep loss.

Now that you have finished this book, you can join a community of people known as cycle breakers. These are the brave folks who have done the challenging work of looking at their past, understanding how it presently shows up, and taking accountability for changing their future. This was no small task, as you now know. Just as trauma is pervasive and compounding, so is healing. Your healing impacts not only you—its positive nature ripples outward and touches every area you come into contact with. If you have children or take care of young kids, you have already given them one of the greatest gifts imaginable—accountability around what is "your stuff to work on" so that the cycle of unintentional parenting and caregiving, as Dr. Vincent Felitti (1998) called it, doesn't continue. With or without children, consider your healing as positively touching anyone you encounter. Being able to work through my stuff led me to a profession that allows me help others, which eventually led me to write this book for all of you. Who can say what your healing will bring to the world.

What *is* clear, however, is that by healing your relational childhood trauma, you are part of a global health strategy (Metzler 2017). Healthy people create more healthy people, who build healthy communities, and pour into a healthier world. By getting the support you needed from this book, you are stopping the cycle of harm from repeating—mentally, physically, and emotionally.

Perhaps you have healed from your parents' high academic expectations of you by building self-esteem outside of work, and learned to manage your stress by engaging in more self-care. At your latest doctor's visit, you are told that your blood pressure issue has gone down significantly. At home, your wife continually says she comes last on your list of priorities. As a result, you take your healing into your own hands and work to change how you show up in the world. You even teach your young son about the importance of work–life balance, including self-care and coping skills, and subsequently he doesn't experience any chronic stress or blood pressure issues in his adult life. He prioritizes weekly date nights with his partner and enjoys fulfilling relationships and hobbies outside of work. He may never know what it took to get him to this place, but you and I do.

As author and wellness educator Alexandra Elle (2022) says, "When you choose to heal yourself, you actively choose to heal the generations after you." This is brave work you have done, are doing, and will continue to do for the rest of your life. If only the positive impact of our healing were simple to recognize. In truth, we rarely know exactly what harm we prevented by healing. What we do know, though, is that by treating yourself more kindly, meeting your own needs, and seeking out satisfying relationships, you are creating a safer, happier, and healthier world. Thank you for that.

Acknowledgments

This book would not have been possible without the support of my loved ones and colleagues. To my editors, Jennye and Madison, for all your thoughtful feedback and guidance. To Wendy, for our early conversations that helped shape this book into what it became today. To my colleagues whom I learn from constantly. To my clients who give me the immense honor of walking alongside them as they break cycles, build partnerships, and uncover their truest selves. To my community, who has held me through my own healing, shepherding me into becoming my truest self and giving me the strength and fortitude to share my gifts with the world.

References

Albom, M. 2003. *The Five People You Meet in Heaven*, 1st ed. New York: Random House.

Ainsworth, M. 1989. "Attachments Beyond Infancy." *The American Psychologist* 44(4): 709–716.

Bachert, A. 2023. "Complex PTSD Triggers In Relationships." *Charlie Health*. https://www.charliehealth.com/post/complex-ptsd-triggers-in-relationships.

Bassam, K., T. Lecomte, G. Fortin, M. Masse, P. Therien, V. Bouchard, M. Chapleau, K. Paquin, and S. G. Hofmann. 2013. "Mindfulness-Based Therapy: A Comprehensive Meta-Analysis." *Clinical Psychology Review* 33(6): 763–771.

Bennett, M. 2021. "Assertive vs. Aggressive Communication in the Workplace." *Niagara Institute*, October 7. https://www.niagara institute.com/blog/assertive-vs-aggressive-communication.

Benson, K. 2023. "The Protest-Withdraw Pattern: Unraveling Emotional Disconnect in Relationships." https://www.kylebenson.net/protest-withdraw.

Bourbeau, L. 2002. *Heal Your Wounds and Find Your True Self: Finally, a Book That Explains Why It's So Hard Being Yourself*. Twin Lakes, WI: Lotus Press.

Bowlby, J. 1979a. *The Making and Breaking of Affectional Bonds*. London: Tavistock Publications.

———. 1979b. "On Knowing What You Are Not Supposed to Know and Feeling What You Are Not Supposed to Feel." *Canadian Journal of Psychiatry* 24(5): 403–408.

Centre for Addiction and Mental Health (CAMH). n.d "Trauma." CAMH. https://www.camh.ca/en/health-info/mental-illness-and-addiction-index/trauma.

Child Welfare Information Gateway. 2022. "Definitions of Child Abuse and Neglect." US Department of Health and Human Services, Administration for Children and Families, Children's Bureau. https://www.childwelfare.gov/topics/systemwide/laws-policies/statutes/define.

Cleveland Clinic. 2024. "What Is the Fight, Flight, Freeze, or Fawn Response?" July 22. https://health.clevelandclinic.org/what-happens-to-your-body-during-the-fight-or-flight-response.

CPTSD Foundation. n.d. "What Is Complex Post-Traumatic Stress Disorder?" https://cptsdfoundation.org/what-is-complex-post-traumatic-stress-disorder-cptsd.

Coan, J. A., H. S. Schaefer, and R. J. Davidson. 2006. "Lending a Hand: Social Regulation of the Neural Response to Threat." *Psychological Science* 12: 1032–1039.

Creasey, G. 2002. "Associations Between Working Models of Attachment and Conflict Management Behavior in Romantic Couples." *Journal of Counseling Psychology* 49(3): 365–375.

Culatta, E., J. Clay-Warner, K. M. Boyle, and A. Oshri. 2020. "Sexual Revictimization: A Routine Activity Theory Explanation." *Journal of Interpersonal Violence* 35(15–16): 2800–2824.

DiLillo, D., J. Peugh, K. Walsh, J. Panuzio, E. Trask, and S. Evans. 2009. "Child Maltreatment History Among Newlywed Couples: A Longitudinal Study of Marital Outcomes and Mediating Pathways." *Journal of Consulting and Clinical Psychology* 77 (4): 680–92.

Elle, A. 2022. *How We Heal: Uncover Your Power and Set Yourself Free.* San Francisco: Chronicle Books.

Felitti, V. J., R. F. Anda, D. Nordenberg, D. F. Williamson, A. M. Spitz, V. Edwards, M. P. Koss, and J. S. Marks. 1998. "Relationship of Childhood Abuse and Household Dysfunction to Many of the Leading Causes of Death in Adults: The Adverse Childhood Experiences (ACE) Study." *American Journal of Preventive Medicine* 256: 774–86.

Felsen, I. 2017. "Adult-Onset Trauma and Intergenerational Transmission: Integrating Empirical Data and Psychoanalytic Theory." *Psychoanalysis, Self and Context* 12(1): 60–77.

Fereidooni, F., J. K. Daniels, and M. J. J. Lommen. 2024. "Childhood Maltreatment and Revictimization: A Systematic Literature Review." *Trauma, Violence, and Abuse* 25(1): 291–305.

Ferguson, S. 2021. "What Is Relational Trauma? An Overview." *Psych Central.* https://psychcentral.com/ptsd/what-is-relational-trauma.

Gass, R., and J. Ansara. 2015. "Managing Your Triggers Toolkit." Mediators Beyond Borders. https://mediatorsbeyondborders.org/wp-content/uploads/2020/01/managing-your-triggers-toolkit.pdf.

Germer, C. K., and K. D. Neff. 2015. "Cultivating Self-Compassion in Trauma Survivors." In *Mindfulness-Oriented Interventions for Trauma: Integrating Contemplative Practices,* edited by V. M. Follette, J. Briere, D. Rozelle, J. W. Hopper, and D. I. Rome. New York: Guilford Press.

Gottman, J. 2011. *The Science of Trust: Emotional Attunement for Couples.* New York: W. W. Norton.

Gottman, J., J. S. Gottman, and J. DeClaire. 2006. *Ten Lessons to Transform Your Marriage.* New York: Crown Publishers.

Gottman, J., and N. Silver. 1999. *The Seven Principles for Making Marriages Work.* New York: Three Rivers Press.

Greene, C. A., L. Haisley, C. Wallace, and J. D. Ford. 2020. "Intergenerational Effects of Childhood Maltreatment: A Systematic Review of the Parenting Practices of Adult Survivors of Childhood Abuse, Neglect, and Violence." *Clinical Psychology Review* 80: 101891.

Guy-Evans, O. 2023. "Fight, Flight, Freeze, or Fawn: How We Respond to Threats." *Simply Psychology.* https://www.simplypsychology.org/fight-flight-freeze-fawn.html.

Hall-Flavin, D. 2024. "What Is Passive Aggressive Behavior? What Are Some of the Signs?" Mayo Clinic. https://www.mayoclinic.org/healthy-lifestyle/adult-health/expert-answers/passive-aggressive-behavior/faq-20057901.

Hemphill, P. 2024. *What It Takes to Heal: How Transforming Ourselves Can Change the World.* New York: Random House.

Herman, J. L. 1992. "Complex PTSD: A Syndrome in Survivors of Prolonged and Repeated Trauma." *Journal of Traumatic Stress* 5(3): 377–391.

Hill, C. 2020. *Assertiveness Training: How to Stand Up for Yourself, Boost Your Confidence, and Improve Assertive Communication Skills.* Chase Hill Books.

Hopkin, M. 2004. "Link Proved Between Senses and Memory." *Nature.* https://doi.org/10.1038/news040524-12.

Johnson, S. M. 2004. *The Practice of Emotionally Focused Couple Therapy: Creating Connection,* 2nd ed. New York: Brunner-Routledge.

Lahousen, T., H. F. Unterrainer, and H. P. Kapfhammer. 2019. "Psychobiology of Attachment and Trauma: Some General Remarks From a Clinical Perspective." *Frontiers in Psychiatry* 10: 914.

Lavner J. A., B. R. Karney, and T. N. Bradbury. 2016. "Does Couples' Communication Predict Marital Satisfaction, or Does Marital Satisfaction Predict Communication?" *Journal of Marriage and Family* 78(3): 680–694.

Levine, A., and R. Heller. 2010. *Attached: The New Science of Adult Attachment and How It Can Help You Find—And Keep—Love.* New York: TarcherPerigee.

Li, S., F. Zhao, and G. Yu. 2019. "Childhood Maltreatment and Intimate Partner Violence Victimization: A Meta-Analysis." *Child Abuse and Neglect* 88: 212–224.

Main, M., and J. Solomon. 1990. "Procedures for Identifying Infants as Disorganized/Disoriented During the Ainsworth Strange Situation." In *Attachment in the Preschool Years: Theory, Research, and Intervention,* edited by M. T. Greenberg, D. Cicchetti, and E. M. Cummings. Chicago: University of Chicago Press.

Maslow, A. H. 1943. "A Theory of Human Motivation." *Psychological Review* 50(4): 370–396.

Merrick, M. T., D. C. Ford, K. A. Ports, and A. S. Guinn. 2018. "Prevalence of Adverse Childhood Experiences From the 2011–2014 Behavioral Risk Factor Surveillance System in 23 States." *JAMA Pediatrics* 172(11): 1038–1044.

Merrick, M. T., D. C. Ford, K. A. Ports, A. S. Guinn, J. Chen, J. Klevens, et al. 2019. "Vital Signs: Estimated Proportion of Adult Health Problems Attributable to Adverse Childhood Experiences and Implications for Prevention—25 States, 2015–2017." *Morbidity and Mortality Weekly Report* 68: 999–1005.

Metzler, M., M. T. Merrick, J. Klevens, K. A. Ports, and D. C. Ford. 2017. "Adverse Childhood Experiences and Life Opportunities: Shifting the Narrative." *Children and Youth Services Review* 72: 141–149.

Nelson, C. A., R. D. Scott, Z. A. Bhutta, N. B. Harris, A. Danese, and M. Samara. 2020. "Adversity in Childhood Is Linked to Mental and Physical Health Throughout Life." *BMJ (Clinical Research Ed.)* 371: m3048.

Newport Academy. 2017. "How Relational Trauma Impacts Teen Mental Health, Social Connections, and Self Esteem." September 1. https://www.newportacademy.com/resources/mental-health/relational-trauma.

Nummenmaa, L., E. Glerean, R. Hari, and J. K. Hietanen. 2014. "Bodily Maps of Emotions." *Proceedings of the National Academy of Sciences of the United States of America* 111(2): 646–651.

Pharaon, V. 2023. *The Origins of You: How Breaking Family Patterns Can Liberate the Way We Live and Love.* New York: G. P. Putnam's Sons.

Piaget, J. 1962. "The Stages of the Intellectual Development of the Child." *Bulletin of the Menninger Clinic* 26(3): 120–128.

Pipas, M., and M. Jaradat. 2010. "Assertive Communication Skills." *Annales Universitatis Apulensis Series Oeconomica* 12: 649–656.

Pressman, T. 2019. *Deconstructing Anxiety: The Journey from Fear to Fulfillment.* Lanham, MD: Rowman and Littlefield.

Rizvi, S. F. I., and N. N. Najam. 2014. "Parental Psychological Abuse Toward Children and Mental Health Problems in Adolescence." *Pakistan Journal of Medical Sciences* 30(2): 256–260.

Robertson, K. 2005. "Active Listening: More Than Just Paying Attention." *Australian Family Physician* 34(12): 1053–1055.

Robinson, L., J. Segal, and J. Jaffe. 2024. "Attachment Styles and How They Affect Adult Relationships." *Help Guide*, June 20. https://www.helpguide.org/relationships/social-connection/attachment-and-adult-relationships.

Rynfield, R. 2019. "Why Is Complex PTSD Not Included in the DSM?" Sabino Recovery. https://www.sabinorecovery.com/why-is-complex-ptsd-not-in-the-dsm.

Saxe, G. N., B. H. Ellis, and A. D. Brown. 2015. *Trauma Systems Therapy for Children and Teens*, 2nd ed. New York: Guilford Press.

Schreiber, R. E., and J. C. Veilleux. 2022. "The Self-Invalidation Due to Emotion Scale: Development and Psychometric Properties." *Psychological Assessment* 34(10): 937–951.

Siegel, D. J., and T. P. Bryson. 2012. *The Whole-Brain Child: 12 Revolutionary Strategies to Nurture Your Child's Developing Mind.* New York: Bantam Books.

Simpson, J. A., and W. S. Rholes. 2017. "Adult Attachment, Stress, and Romantic Relationships." *Current Opinion in Psychology* 13: 19–24.

Simpson, J. A., W. S. Rholes, and D. Phillips. 1996. "Conflict in Close Relationships: An Attachment Perspective." *Journal of Personality and Social Psychology* 71: 899–914.

Sjöblom, M., K. Öhrling, M. Prellwitz, and C. Kostenius. 2016. "Health Throughout the Lifespan: The Phenomenon of the Inner Child Reflected in Events During Childhood Experienced by Older Persons." *International Journal of Qualitative Studies on Health and Well-Being* 11: 31486.

Swedo, E. A., M. V. Aslam, L. L. Dahlberg, P. H. Niolon, A. S. Guinn, T. R. Simon, and J. A. Mercy. 2023. "Prevalence of Adverse Childhood Experiences Among U.S. Adults—Behavioral Risk Factor Surveillance System, 2011–2020." *Morbidity and Mortality Weekly Report* 72: 707–715.

Tanasugarn, A. 2022. "The Common Effects of Complex Relational Trauma: The Patterns That Replay Childhood Trauma in Our Adult Relationships." *Psychology Today*, June 24. https://www.psychologytoday.com/us/blog/understanding-ptsd/202206/the-common-effects-complex-relational-trauma.

US Department of Veterans Affairs. n.d. "PTSD: National Center for PTSD." https://www.ptsd.va.gov/professional/treat/essentials/complex_ptsd.asp.

Van der Kolk, B. A. 2014. *The Body Keeps the Score: Brain, Mind, and Body in the Healing of Trauma.* New York: Viking.

Melissa Fulgieri, LCSW, is a social worker, adjunct professor, speaker, and author based in New York, NY. She owns a private therapy practice, helping individuals and couples live and love more authentically. She teaches at Fordham Graduate School of Social Service, and Long Island University Graduate School of Health Professions. She has written features for top publications such as *Authority Magazine, Women's Health,* and *Bustle.* She is author of *Couples Therapy Activity Book.*

Real change *is* possible

For more than fifty years, New Harbinger has published proven-effective self-help books and pioneering workbooks to help readers of all ages and backgrounds improve mental health and well-being, and achieve lasting personal growth. In addition, our spirituality books offer profound guidance for deepening awareness and cultivating healing, self-discovery, and fulfillment.

Founded by psychologist Matthew McKay and Patrick Fanning, New Harbinger is proud to be an independent, employee-owned company. Our books reflect our core values of integrity, innovation, commitment, sustainability, compassion, and trust. Written by leaders in the field and recommended by therapists worldwide, New Harbinger books are practical, accessible, and provide real tools for real change.

 **newharbinger**publications

MORE BOOKS from
NEW HARBINGER PUBLICATIONS

THE UPWARD SPIRAL

Using Neuroscience to Reverse the Course of Depression, One Small Change at a Time

978-1626251205 / US $18.95

ADULT SURVIVORS OF TOXIC FAMILY MEMBERS

Tools to Maintain Boundaries, Deal with Criticism, and Heal from Shame After Ties Have Been Cut

978-1684039289 / US $19.95

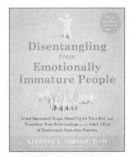

DISENTANGLING FROM EMOTIONALLY IMMATURE PEOPLE

Avoid Emotional Traps, Stand Up for Your Self, and Transform Your Relationships as an Adult Child of Emotionally Immature Parents

978-1648481512 / US $21.95

WIRED FOR LOVE, SECOND EDITION

How Understanding Your Partner's Brain and Attachment Style Can Help You Defuse Conflict and Build a Secure Relationship

978-1648482960 / US $19.95

ADULT CHILDREN OF EMOTIONALLY IMMATURE PARENTS

How to Heal from Distant, Rejecting, or Self-Involved Parents

978-1626251700 / US $18.95

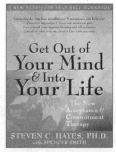

GET OUT OF YOUR MIND AND INTO YOUR LIFE

The New Acceptance and Commitment Therapy

978-1572244252 / US $24.95

new**harbinger**publications

1-800-748-6273 / newharbinger.com

(VISA, MC, AMEX / prices subject to change without notice)

Follow Us 📷 📘 ❤ 🇽 ▶ 📌 💼 ♪ ⑥

Don't miss out on new books from New Harbinger.
Subscribe to our email list at **newharbinger.com/subscribe** 🖱

Did you know there are **free tools** you can download for this book?

Free tools are things like **worksheets**, **guided meditation exercises**, and **more** that will help you get the most out of your book.

You can download free tools for this book—whether you bought or borrowed it, in any format, from any source—from the New Harbinger website. All you need is a NewHarbinger.com account. Just use the URL provided in this book to view the free tools that are available for it. Then, click on the "download" button for the free tool you want, and follow the prompts that appear to log in to your NewHarbinger.com account and download the material.

You can also save the free tools for this book to your **Free Tools Library** so you can access them again anytime, just by logging in to your account! Just look for this button on the book's free tools page.

+ Save this to my free tools library

If you need help accessing or downloading free tools, visit **newharbinger.com/faq** or contact us at **customerservice@newharbinger.com**.